Endorsements

Freeman's life stretches from an Amish home and school in rural Ohio to inner city Philadelphia's universities and churches. And you wonder. How far can a person stretch? Without breaking. How can roots sink deep in black earth--and cement sidewalks? In homogeneous rural communities--and multi-ethnic urban ones? Discover the "secret sauce" that flavors this rich, multi-faceted life!

Jewel Showalter works in Communications & Development at Rosedale Bible College after a lifetime of cross-cultural church work in both rural and urban settings.

Freeman's life story is an inspiring reminder that clarity about God's call on our lives can propel us through unimaginable life transformation. If a humble Amish boy from rural Ohio can become a university professor and a pastor/bishop in a major urban center, then with God anything is possible!

Keith Weaver, Retired Bishop and Former Moderator of LMC

We are all on a journey. Freeman is inviting us to join him as he reflects on his journey from an agrarian Amish lad to an urbane urbanite, from being a resident of a homogeneous culture to living in a very heterogeneous setting, through various occupations and geographical settings across several continents, all led by the ultimate tour guide, the Lord himself. His story is told with wonder and respect, acknowledging the impact of his heritage and mentors, all of whom God used to lead him to the city of Brotherly Love, in anticipation of becoming a permanent resident of the eternal Holy City.

Carl Horning, Retired Bishop of LMC

Freeman has spent much, if not all, of his adult life for the peace and welfare of the city. Leaving the safety net of Plain City, Ohio, he recognized that privilege follows us wherever we go. Over four decades, I have witnessed Freeman leverage this privilege for kingdom-building—using his power, authority, influence, and networks to work for the peace and prosperity of the city, the local community, and the church he so passionately loves. Freeman Miller's story, like each of our own stories, is still being written, so may his example contained herein inspire us all to build, plant, multiply, and work for the peace of our own communities.

Leonard M. Dow, former pastor of OCMC

From the slow buggies of an agricultural Amish community in Ohio to the rapid subways of his beloved multi-cultural city of Philadelphia, Freeman Miller's life story is unique and inspiring. While holding deep respect for his home community, Freeman, Naomi, and their family embody the prophet Jeremiah's vision of seeking "peace for the city."

Loren Swartzendruber, seminary classmate and President Emeritus, Eastern Mennonite University

Freeman is a dear friend and colleague, and I am thrilled that he has written his unique life story. Freeman and I met in the 1990's while working together at the Philadelphia campus of Messiah College (now Messiah University). The Philly campus was a special place where students from the main campus in Grantham, PA, would come for an urban immersion, taking classes at Temple University and getting a taste of life in the big, colorful city. I was born, raised, and have lived in Philadelphia all my life. Temple was my alma mater, and so Philly was Philly. It was home. Nothing special. But Freeman was born and raised Amish, rural, and viewed the city through a very different and enthusiastic lens. That was the beginning of our friendship. I was amazed by his joy and hope for my city.

It is a luminous journey across worlds that are too often kept separate: Amish farms and city streets, rural and urban classrooms, Nigerian schoolhouses, and diverse Mennonite houses of faith. Filled with Anabaptist conviction and the noisy demands of public leadership, with humility, warmth, and presence, Freeman invites readers into a life shaped by unexpected calls and a willingness to say yes. This memoir is more than a personal story; it is a testimony to faithful curiosity, courageous transition, and the enduring power of community. Readers interested in faith, race, education, mission, and the lived practice of unity in diversity will find this memoir deeply moving and radically transformative, a life well lived, thoughtfully told, and generously shared.

Calenthia Dowdy, PhD, former college professor and director at Philadelphia Fight

In *From Farming to Philadelphia*, Freeman J. Miller recounts Messiah College's bold venture to extend its educational mission into the heart of Philadelphia through the Messiah College Philadelphia Campus (MCPC). This memoir captures both the vision and the lived reality of that endeavor—an initiative in which Freeman played a defining role as educator, administrator, and guide to generations of students. As Provost during much of this period, I had the privilege of working closely with Freeman to help shape Messiah's presence on North Broad Street and to strengthen its partnership with Temple University. His story invites readers into the challenges, hopes, and transformative encounters that marked MCPC's life at Broad and Diamond. Readers of this memoir will gain not only a clear window into the history and purpose of MCPC, but also a deeper appreciation for the life of a faithful Anabaptist educator whose passion for Christian witness in the city profoundly shaped the lives of students who had the privilege of studying with him.

Randall Basinger, Provost and Professor of Philosophy Emeritus, Messiah University

Bishop Freeman and I share a deep history rooted in our upbringing in the rural, white, Amish Mennonite community of Plain City, Ohio, and in our present lives in the diverse, multicultural city of Philadelphia. When I moved to Philadelphia in 1994, my mother, fearful of my move to the big city, introduced me to Freeman, her former teacher at Plainview School, who had moved to Philadelphia two decades earlier. Freeman played a crucial role in helping me adapt to this unfamiliar urban environment by introducing me to an African American, former Messiah College student who became both my roommate and lifelong friend. Over the years, our worlds have continued to intersect through the small, diverse Mennonite community in Philadelphia. Freeman has consistently been a voice of hope, inspiring me personally as I considered leaving my job at Temple to help found the Oxford Circle Christian Community Development Association (OCCCDA). In my professional work as a social worker, voices of hope are essential to continuing Christ's mission of serving the "least of these". Freeman's story exemplifies this hope, serving as a model for loving others as Jesus did, regardless of differences in race, culture, or background.

Anita Lyndaker Studer, founder and former director of Oxford Circle Christian Community Development Association

From Farming to Philadelphia is a beautifully written tribute to a life shaped by faith, resilience, and openness to change. Bishop Freeman Miller's journey from rural Ohio to Africa and then to the vibrant center of Philadelphia tells an inspiring story of growth and hope. His reflections emphasize personal development through significant transitions and remind us of the power of community, the richness of diversity, and the ongoing presence of God's grace. This memoir seeks to motivate readers of all backgrounds to trust their calling and discover purpose wherever their paths may take them.

Nelson Okanya, former president, Eastern Mennonite Missions and Leadership Consultant

The Eastern Mennonite Seminary class of 1975 chose Freeman Miller as its president. He already had international experience, in addition to undergraduate work at a State University, during the Vietnam War. Freeman pushed us academically and urged us to take the relevance of the Christian message into our times. Following seminary, he and Naomi headed for Philadelphia to immerse themselves in urban life and ministry. Their lives gave meaning to "missional" before it was a thing. In these pages, we find the account of an energetic soul who has shared an enthusiasm for following Jesus over the past 50+ years!

Owen E. Burkholder, fellow seminarian, retired pastor, and conference moderator, Virginia Mennonite Conference

I have known Freeman Miller for over 30 years, as a minister and bishop for the Philadelphia District of LMC, and as a valued member of my church. Freeman Miller is a connector of people and a collector of stories. His own story is one of moving from the sheltered community of the Old Order Amish to the inner city of Philadelphia, adapting to different cultures, languages, perspectives, and values. It is an important story of making friends and building connections across these vast differences while staying vitally connected to his home community, and it offers important lessons for people today. In a climate where people are quick to separate across ideological lines, Freeman's story shows how openness to the leading of God and curiosity towards others leads to a much richer experience of cultivating and keeping friendships

Lynn Parks, Lead Pastor, Oxford Circle Mennonite Church

FROM FARMING TO PHILADELPHIA

FROM FARMING TO PHILADELPHIA

The Global Journey of an Amish Man

FREEMAN J. MILLER

First Printing, 2026
Published by Santos Books LLC, Conrad L. Kanagy, Publisher
ISBN: 979-8-9948938-1-4
Cover design: Ron Tinsley

CONTENTS

For My Grandchildren

ACKNOWLEDGMENTS

To God and the amazing multitude of people he brought into my life–those mentioned and unmentioned in my memoir–I owe an eternal debt of gratitude. Without them, this book would not exist, nor would I exist to write it. They all helped shape and sustain my life, my character.

Special thanks to my dear wife Naomi, my soulmate, lifelong urban ministry partner and perceptive proofreader, and to our daughters Janelle, Rhonda, and Gwen and their families, who helped create this improbable narrative.

My sincere gratitude to the author group at Santos Books, who helped shape the final manuscript, especially Conrad Kanagy, Publisher. A loud shout out to all my former students at Plainview, Johnstown, Crowther, and Messiah. You helped me stay on the cutting edge of discovery and hope for the future. To the beautiful souls at Diamond Street, Oxford Circle, and all the other churches I was privileged to work with, at home and abroad, thank you for keeping the faith alive! God bless you.

I wanted to write the story of my life, not only as a memoir for my children and grandchildren–important as that was–but also as a testimonial to the amazing grace of our awesome God, who sees the end from the beginning. Looking back over my life was an exercise in counting my blessings, only to realize that they are far too numerous to collect in a single book. As the contemporary Christian song says, "God, I'm still counting my blessings...But I can't count that high!" If anyone tries to connect the many improbable pieces of my patchwork quilt of a life and attribute it to my intelligence, will, or intentional human design, I challenge them to do so without detecting the fingerprints of a Master Artist at work behind the scenes all the way through. You will likely discover that he's weaving your story and mine together.

All memory is selective. No two people remember a shared event exactly alike. I am pulling my life story from my memory bank and apologize in advance to any readers who remember the events differently from how I do. That is to be expected. That is part of being human. As we share our stories, they bind us together in the great human family, enriched by our uniqueness and similarities, even in the way we "re-member" history.

Grab your favorite beverage, curl up in a comfortable chair, and join me on the journey of my life. Prepare to be amazed and encouraged, as you watch God lead our family and me through the many ups and downs, the curves and cliffs, the storms and sunshine which are sure to meet all of us on the highway of life. Prepare also to embrace the city as a viable and vibrant habitat for humanity, whether you grew up rural, urban, or suburban. The city is God's idea; in fact, he's building one right now. Let's join each other and our neighbors in journeying ever onward and upward together. *Excelsior!*

Freeman J. Miller

Spring, 2026

FOREWORD

In the well-known passage from Jeremiah 29, we read God's instructions to the Israelites during their Babylonian exile—a time of profound upheaval and displacement. God calls them to settle in a community not their own, yet precisely where God has placed them. The message is clear:

"Build homes, and plan to stay. Plant gardens and eat the food they produce. Marry and have children. Then find spouses for them so that you may have many grandchildren. Multiply! Do not dwindle away! And work for the peace and prosperity of the city where I sent you into exile. Pray to the Lord for it, for its welfare will determine your welfare.

These instructions—build, plant, multiply, and work for peace—are not just ancient commands. They are a blueprint for faithful Christ-like living, even in unfamiliar places. Each directive carries deep meaning:

- **Build houses and settle down.** This is a call to put down roots, to make a long-term commitment, even when circumstances are uncertain.
- **Plant gardens and eat their produce.** Planting is an act of hope, a sign that you believe in the future and are willing to invest in it.
- **Marry, have children, and multiply.** This is about legacy—embracing the community, its people, traditions, and challenges as your own.

- **Work for the peace and prosperity of the city.** True peace requires solidarity with the "least, lost, and last"—those most vulnerable to violence and injustice. It means using your position to uplift others, as Jesus taught.

In Freeman Miller's life, these principles are not just ideals—they are embodied realities. Like Jeremiah before him, Freeman responded to God's call by relocating, residing, and settling down in the city of Philadelphia. Freeman and Naomi didn't just move to the city; they invested a lifetime of time, talent, and treasure! Their years on Carlisle Street in North Philly were marked by deep relationships—extending and receiving love within a tight-knit community.

Freeman's commitment to mentorship, church planting, and community development has shaped countless lives and the Mennonite church in Philadelphia. He supported me during my early years as a pastor at Oxford Circle Mennonite Church and later I would follow in his footsteps as one of the bishops in the ethnically diverse Philadelphia District of LMC. But I am just one among many! Freeman's influence spans generations, cultures and communities —church planters, bishops, pastors, worship leaders, teachers, professors, social workers, financial professionals, realtors, tradespeople, politicians, entrepreneurs, bankers, medical professionals, and more have all been touched by his guidance and encouragement.

And it is important to note that Freeman and Naomi took Jeremiah's call to "multiply" very seriously! Their legacy begins with their three daughters, sons-in-law, nine grandchildren, and now a great-grandchild. Each, in their own way, carries forward the Miller legacy: love of God in Christ, love of the city and your neighbor, love of the church and the community they serve.

Perhaps most profoundly, Freeman has spent much, if not all, of his adult life for the peace and welfare of the city. Leaving the safety net of Plain City Ohio, he recognized that privilege follows us wherever we go. Over four decades, I have witnessed Freeman leverage this privilege for kingdom-building purposes—using his power, authority, influence, and networks to work for the peace and prosperity of the city, the local community, and for the church he so passionately loves. Freeman Miller's story, like each of our own stories, is still being written, so may his example contained herein inspire us all to build, plant, multiply, and work for the peace of our own communities. *Selah*

Leonard M. Dow

VP of Church and Community Development, Everence Financial

Former pastor of Oxford Circle Mennonite Church, Philadelphia

I Push My Way Into the World

I was born in Plain City, Ohio. I could have been born anywhere in the world, but I emerged near a tiny, plain city on a smooth plain in a small community of plain people called the Amish. They look plain and simple to an outside observer, but they are quite the opposite from an insider's perspective. They are as interesting, varied, and complex as any group of people you will meet anywhere. If you've visited the small town I'm talking about, you know it sits on flat land filled with small farms and businesses. If you are used to the soaring majesty of mountain peaks and fertile valleys, you may be tempted to think that life on the flat farms of Madison County in Ohio must be boring. But looks can be deceiving. I had an exciting childhood, rich and full of lively activity, fun, and hard work, creating thousands of cherished memories. There was even drama in this close-knit rural community, like the night my Amish farmer-preacher Grandpa Miller lost his arm–and almost his life–on the dining room table in the farmhouse near midnight after harvesting corn. But that comes later in this story.

I was born on a typical fall day in the middle of September. September 12, to be exact. Farmers were bringing in the harvest, filling silos, husking or picking corn, filling the barns and silos with all the feed and fodder the animals would need to survive the winter. The smell of burning leaves may have filled the air, as there were many leaves to be raked and burned at the edge of the well-manicured lawn. A few flowers still bloomed in the lush gardens, now turning brown, and the martin houses sat sadly empty, bits of straw and fur still dangling out of the nest holes, as the purple martins had flown south for the winter. Buggies (horse-drawn carriages), tractors, horses pulling wagons, and an occasional bicycle passed by on the road, as our little community got itself ready for fall and school. There was apple butter to be made, last-minute butchering to be done, provisions to be laid up in the basement, and preparations to be made for hosting the Amish church service at our house. Church families in our district would take turns hosting the biweekly services, and our turn came around once a year, usually in the fall.

On that very pastoral day in 1942, I decided to push my way into the world and say my first hello, but it came out mostly as a wail. Perhaps I was feeling the pain of World War II, raging at the time. My Uncle John was serving as a conscientious objector in CPS camps in my father's stead, so that my father could be at home for my birth and to keep the home place going.

The Bible would say I opened my mother's womb (Luke 2:23KJV), as I was her firstborn child, born to a shy and petite 22-year old Amish girl, married not quite two years to a young Amish man who had just turned 22 a mere eleven days before (I guess I was his birthday present). My dad was the youngest son in a large family, who, as custom would have it, had "inherited" the task of taking over the family farm on the Amish Pike, whether he wanted to be a farmer or not. I believe they were "ready" for me, as early marriages, large families, and the many demands of farm life were normal in my community. But who can ever really be *ready* for the birth of a child? Especially when it's the first one. My grandparents were living in the Doddy ("Grandpa") Haus right next to the big house. I instantly became part of a large extended "family," with neighbors, cousins, and other Amish families clustered close together on farms surrounding Plain City. What a perfect setting for me to present my curious little self to the world! As I hinted earlier, there was hardly ever a dull moment, even though the "English" people driving by on the road in their fancy, shiny cars would naively look at us and think we were "frozen" in a 16th-century way of life, subsisting on apple butter and corn bread with almost no modern amenities, certainly with very little fun–a hard, routine life, full of daily chores done mostly by hand. That is why one should read outsiders' descriptions of Amish life with a grain of salt and try to get first-hand insider perspectives whenever possible.

I was born at home in Mom and Dad's bedroom, with Grandma and Aunt Martha standing by to assist my mother and Dr. Ingmire in my laborious entrance into this life as a curious and healthy little boy. The Amish had this down to a science: when the labor pains were getting to the right stage, somebody would quickly hop on a bike or a buggy and go to the nearest farm with a telephone to call the doctor, who would know by now just how soon to appear in his gleaming car from town. The neighbors would see it and think, "Oh yes, the time has come!" And before noon, the word would spread throughout the community, even though the Amish did not have telephones, electricity, or other modern means of communication. The following week, everybody in the Amish world all over the country would know of my birth, for the local scribe would faithfully record all such important events in the national Amish newspaper, called simply, *The Budget.* It still exists today and continues to serve the purpose of keeping Amish communities informed and connected.

Almost every Amish community in the world has a *Budget* "scribe," whose job it is to collect all the important information each week and submit it to the editor for publication in that week's edition. Next to the Bible, this is the most faithfully-read publication by almost all Amish people–especially the columns about the people and places where one has relatives or knows somebody. So it was expected at church, family, or social gatherings to hear, as someone was sharing the latest news, "Yes, I read that in *The Budget.*" The Amish were way ahead of their time by creating their own "Facebook" to build and maintain virtual communities with the limited technology they had. This is another facet of

Amish life, often little understood; the Amish were both way "behind" the times and yet in some ways "ahead" of the times. They still are, as numerous recent studies suggest.

So you might say that my arrival on the planet made world history! How many people can look back with confidence and know that their birth was announced in a nationwide newspaper, that they were welcomed into a close-knit home and community which was expressly set up to assure mutual aid and lifelong support to its members, and which had succeeded in preserving its faith and heritage for 250 years against all odds in a modern world? This idyllic description of Amish culture doesn't always live up to the ideal, as any insider can tell you, but it does provide a generalized context for me to begin telling my childhood story.

I didn't know it then, but I know it now, that Mom and Dad would care for me with utmost love, that Grandma and Grandpa Miller were always nearby–as were Aunt Martha, Aunt Fran, Aunt Mary, my Hostetler grandparents, and all my aunts, uncles, cousins, and relatives–indeed, the entire Amish community, to stand together through all the ups and downs of life. Soon, I would also almost certainly have numerous siblings, true to Amish custom. Rugged individualism was almost unheard of in our context, where my business was everyone's business and vice versa, bound together in a covenant community of mutual support and accountability.

So even though we had to heat water on the stove for our baths (in a zinc tub in the pantry), chop wood or carry coal for heating our houses, draw water from a pump, and use an outhouse rain or shine for our toilet needs, our house was always warm, the food was plentiful (*too plentiful!*) and delicious, work was endless, and so was love. God and community were taken for granted, and you grew up absorbing the local mores with your mother's milk (unless you were bottle-fed). I was dressed in little homemade Amish clothes (infant girls and boys both wore dresses), wrapped in warm blankets, and carried by my parents in a buggy to the church services held every two weeks in someone's house, and all the women would ooh and aah over what a cute baby Joe and Edna had! Look at those eyes, and that nose–just like his dad! And on and on. There was a room somewhere in the house where my mom could take me to nurse or if I cried during the three-hour German worship service. We learned soon enough how to hold still and sit for those grueling hours on backless benches, looking forward to the bowl of crackers, pretzels, or cookies quietly passed around midway through the service, and dreading the day when we would be too old to enjoy this little repast meant only for the youngest among us.

All in all, this was not a bad way to be welcomed into the world. Even though the Amish sometimes used midwives, most births happened in the home with the local doctor supervising the birth. I am quite sure my birth was typical for that time and place. Years later, my younger siblings were born in a local hospital, as the Amish began to use more and more of the medical services available.

And so begins the story of one life–mine. It would become an amazing adventure, as we shall see. Looking back on one's life can lead to the realization that every life in the world since Adam and Eve has been unique, full of meaning, and connects all of us to one another in the human family. Apparently, you and I are related, like it or not. Every life becomes a work of art when placed inside a frame, for that is the nature of frames. Master artists and storytellers are often able to put all the small frames together inside a larger frame, revealing an even greater work of art, a masterpiece. Think, for example, of the ceiling over the Sistine Chapel.

When you stop to consider, every story ever written, every photo, every piece of history, every work of art, every building, every city, is about people and their context–people created by an omnipotent Creator who decided not only to make everyone in his own image, but to come down, "move into the neighborhood" (Jn 1:14 MSG), live among us, and eventually take us to live in the eternal city with him forever. Perhaps by then I will have time to hear your story, as you are hearing mine now, and realize that every human life is a snapshot of God. Every life story, when woven together by the heavenly Author into his eternal story, becomes part of HisStory. That gives meaning, purpose, and direction to every life, providing ample reason for getting up in the morning, knowing that you are part of something much greater than yourself.

"For we are God's <u>masterpiece</u>. He has created us anew in Christ Jesus, so that we can do the good things he planned for us long ago (Eph 2:10 NLT) The Greek word here translated "masterpiece" is *poiema*, from which our English word "poem" derives, so we are really God's poetry in the world. Poetry attempts to catch our deepest emotions in words. Other works of art–music, sculpture, a farm, a painting, or a pie–capture emotions in other forms as well. One tiny but crucial pronoun from this verse in Ephesians 2 often escapes notice in our fast-paced world--the word "we." There is no "me" without "we."

As I have described my life so far, it may seem all about me. But read it again, and you will see that in the world of the Amish, it is really about "we," and without "we," the "me" has little or no meaning. This aligns well with the worldview of the Hebrew people in the Old Testament and the early church in the New Testament. The point of Paul's Epistle to the church in Ephesus–especially in chapters 2 and 3–is that Paul is trying to put into words God's secret, or "mystery"–only lately revealed to him–that God had intended all along to have Jews and Gentiles (indeed, people from all over the world; see Psalm 87) to become part of this one-and-only family of the one-and-only God! That we Gentiles were not excluded after all; that we have the same access as the covenant people of God. That the truly amazing "masterpiece," "poetry," or "symphony" that God wants to display in the world is his multicultural, international family, united as one in Christ. I can never be God's poetry alone; it is only as the church of Jesus Christ, his family, that reflects the collective and many-faceted "WE" that we can truly make the Master proud of his Masterpiece. (See the prayer of Jesus in John 17.)

Perhaps you think I'm being too "preachy" here. Maybe I am. But I've been a teacher and preacher most of my life. I come from a family of preachers. Every incident can become a sermon, an illustration, or a parable. Parables can be very interesting. I could not honestly tell my life story without reflecting on how God was at work around me, for me, and through me in all of it. I could not have imagined or engineered my improbable life if I had tried.

Here is a photo of my grandfather, "One-armed Amish preacher, Joe Doddy Miller," who lived in the small "Doddy Haus" next to our large homestead. You will be hearing more about him as we go along. He was very instrumental in shaping my life and worldview.

CHAPTER 2

My Early Childhood

My memories of the first few years of my life are rather foggy and sketchy, of course, as most of us do not remember much before the age of two. Perhaps the earliest memory I can pull up is the birth of my sister, Martha, who is several years younger than I am. I remember that I had to go to the "Doddy Haus" (Grandpa House) right next to ours overnight, and I wasn't clear why until the next morning. While it was still dark, I remember hearing the sound of rubber tires leaving our gravel driveway. The sound of rubber tires is decidedly different from steel buggy wheels or wagon wheels on gravel, and that sound always signaled an "intrusion" from the world, since the Amish did not allow rubber tires. I asked my grandparents which car that was, leaving so early in the morning, and they said it was Dr. Ingmire's. Of course, in the mind of a two-year-old, a doctor's visit meant something was wrong, so I was understandably nervous about this news.

After daybreak, however, my fears were allayed when Grandma Miller took me over to the big house and introduced me to my new baby sister! I am still not sure how the doctor knew just when to arrive for the birth of a baby, but somehow, doctors serving Amish communities managed to have a pretty reliable system in place. A new baby always meant an exciting time of transition in the Amish home, because not only was there a new member of the family to include in all daily activities, but for several weeks, a hired maid would live with the family and help with all the added demands of caring for a new baby. So for several weeks, we would have extra mouths to feed, extra chores to do, and new routines to establish. Most of my earliest memories include my sister, and later, other siblings, as they were born, of course. I have very few memories of myself as the only grandchild on my mother's side at that time, but I'll mention a few that stand out as formative experiences in my memory bank.

I cannot remember either of my grandmothers distinctly, but I can share a few vague impressions. My maternal grandmother—Grandma Hostetler—was ill with cancer and died when I was just three years old. The two memories of her that I treasure include a trip or two to a hospital in Cincinnati to see her in her sickbed. On one such visit, I was asked to sing for her, which apparently created quite a stir. I seem to have been able to carry a tune at a very early age, and I had even memorized the first verse of a popular Amish hymn from the little black German hymnal, *Liedersammlung*, used by the youth in hymn sings, with German lyrics sung to popular English tunes. (This book of hymns should not be confused with the traditional thick old Amish hymnal, the *Ausbund,* used for the slow-tune, plaintive German chants in Amish worship services. The *Ausbund* is one of the oldest Christian hymn books still in continuous use. It contains mostly martyr hymns, drawn from Anabaptist persecution and martyrdom in the 1500's and beyond. Amish church singing–chanted in unison–can sound almost funeral-like, reflecting a long history of persecution, suffering, and death.)

While the song I had memorized from the little black book had similar lyrics, the tune was more modern and upbeat. The song which I sang for my terminally ill Grandma Hostetler was "Bedenke, Mensch, das Ende." It must have sounded very cute for a two-year-old, as it brought cheers and smiles from the adults, according to family lore. (I can still sing this song by memory to this day.) In retrospect, it seems like the most unfitting song to sing to my dying grandmother. Loosely translated, the title says, "Consider, O human, your final end." It is an admonition to live a sober and righteous life, for you could die tomorrow. I suppose my grandma smiled with the others, having already considered her life's impending end and having made her peace with God. I hope it cheered her up for at least one day as she lingered in the hospital.

The other faint memory of Grandma Hostetler is one of her coming in from the garden with fresh produce and fixing a lettuce sandwich for me, probably with some bright red radishes on the side to be dipped in salt and eaten with the rest of lunch. I can't remember what she said or what she looked like, but it was a precious snapshot that stays with me. As the oldest and only grandchild on my mother's side for several years, I definitely enjoyed a few special privileges, and my grandparents probably spoiled me. My Hostetler cousins would certainly agree!

One special privilege was spending the night at Grandpa Hostetler's house.

My maternal grandparents lived just about twenty minutes away by bike or by buggy, and we could see their farm across the fields on the Lafayette-Plain City Road. So it was easy to get to their house, and it was indeed special to spend the night with them. I must have slept over while Grandma Hostetler was still alive, but most of my overnight memories are of Grandpa living alone in the big farmhouse.

I remember the sights and sounds of his chilly, dark bedroom. To me, the most important fact was that I got to spend time alone with my grandpa, and that was all that mattered! A special part of any sleepover came the next morning at breakfast, when I was allowed to sit next to "Mose Doddy" (our name for him as his name was Mose Hostetler) and dip my apple butter bread or toast into his coffee, and even sip a little coffee on my own! We bonded deeply—a bond that lasted a lifetime. A breakfast favorite of mine to this day is apple butter bread or toast dipped in coffee, and I almost always think of my grandfather as I enjoy it. I wonder if we will enjoy apple butter toast and coffee in heaven. I also remember helping with chores around the barn and riding his tractor with him. As I grew older, I got to ride to town with him in his horse and buggy and sip milkshakes at the drugstore next to him, perched on high barstools by the marble bar top.

Here is a photo of my grandfather, "Mose Doddy Hostetler." He is sitting on a hickory rocker ("Hecka Shtuhl") surrounded by several of my cousins and my Aunt Martha (Hostetler) Helmuth.

When it comes to my Miller grandparents—the ones living in the little house almost touching ours—I have more memories, as I interacted with them on a daily basis, although again, Grandma Miller died when I was quite young, and I don't remember her very distinctly either. I remember her wooden toy box, her floor-length homemade dresses, and her cheery kitchen. Her face, sadly, has faded into a blur over the years. I don't have a single photo of her. I have photos of both grandfathers–which is curious, since the Amish did not allow photographs–but not a single photo of either grandmother. How did that happen?

I got many of my first life lessons—very important ones, too—at Grandma Miller's knee. She would read Bible stories to me and explain what they meant, and play games that simulated life. For example, we would play "store," with me purchasing items from the toy box and then paying her with real pennies, nickels, and dimes. So I was learning how to count money, spend wisely, and how to do simple math. I remember the mantle clock ticking and striking whenever I was at their house, along with many other warm sounds and smells, especially from the kitchen. I loved helping her bake bread and "snail houses"; there was nothing more delightful than punching down the bread dough and watching it rise, while she baked, ironed, and sewed. There was always a floured surface for shaping the dough into loaves or rolls, and the leftover bits we rolled with apple butter or jelly into little snail-shaped rollups to eat with lunch. I was rather young when Grandma Miller died, and I remember someone at the wake or funeral saying under their breath, "I wonder if he's old enough to understand what's happening?" Apparently, I was.

I must include a sad note here. I referred to the mantle clock in Grandpa and Grandma Miller's living room, which had a gold pendulum that mesmerized me as a kid. I kept wondering just what made that clock tick and strike. I knew that Grandpa Miller wound the clock regularly, but I wondered what was inside that beautiful, mysterious time machine that made it keep time and chime so musically every time another hour had passed. I was delighted that when my grandparents' things were divided up (Naomi and I were living in Nigeria when Joe Doddy died), my family had managed to save the mantle clock for me. When we moved into our house at 2027 N. Carlisle Street in Philadelphia in 1980, I found the perfect place for it—on the mantle above the fireplace in the living room! It was a tangible, daily reminder of my roots, and as the minutes and hours ticked and chimed away, I was reminded of the loving God who had directed our winding adventure from the day I left home to the day we finally settled in Philadelphia.

This would be the place for a happy ending to this part of my story, with plans for this timeless timepiece to be passed on to one of my off-spring someday, were it not for the break-in and robbery that occurred one summer night while I was away at a church-planters retreat. Naomi and the girls were asleep upstairs with the air conditioner running and the doors closed, so they did not find out when the intruders made off with our TV, stereo, and various other replaceable items, along with this most precious family heirloom! So now I know what people mean when they bemoan the loss of possessions but are most saddened by these precious reminders of generations past.

And now I must talk about Grandpa Miller (Joe Doddy). I only realized decades later what an enormous impact both of my grandfathers had on my social and spiritual formation. I now know that, as an impressionable young boy, I internalized a lot more of what my parents and grandparents modeled than I realized at the time. This is no doubt true for most of us as we grow up–that we "learn what we live" by watching our elders–but in my case it takes on added significance as I now firmly believe that my two grandfathers—Amish farmers though they were—played a major part in preparing me mentally and spiritually to leave my rural roots, spend significant time overseas and elsewhere, eventually ending up transplanted and at peace in the heart of Philadelphia. At first, when people kept asking me how an Amish farm boy could be at home in the big city, I was tempted to think there was something different in my character or makeup that allowed me to adjust more easily to change than other people. While that could be true, I now think my grandfathers had a great deal to do with it, along with some key teachers at the Amish/Mennonite school I attended for ten years.

Joe Doddy was no ordinary Amish preacher. Oh yes, he was a farmer like most Amish preachers and had to get up way before dawn to read the Bible and pray. And like other Amish preachers, he was not allowed to take any notes up front to guide him as he preached; in fact, he couldn't even have an open Bible or New Testament to preach from. (Context note: Amish preachers don't have a pulpit. They stand in the open doorway of someone's living room, turning to the left, then right, to roomfuls of adults on backless benches.) Everything had to be "by heart." I remember his comment about how glad he was when he was finally permitted to carry a German New Testament in his suit coat pocket and refer to it as he preached.

In addition, he had lost his left arm in a terrible corn-shredding accident. In the fall of 1913, as a young 34-year-old farmer and father of six young children, he reached into the corn shredder to unclog the blower pipe when his coat sleeve pulled his arm in and mangled it. It was after dark on a Saturday night, and they wanted to quickly finish. He lost a lot of blood, and the doctors had to amputate his arm above the elbow with a meat-cutting saw, lying on the dining room table at midnight. He almost lost his life, but recovered and healed for several weeks before he could begin "normal" life again. He had a harness shop make a leather harness and hook so he could continue with his many duties.

In my mind, two traits set him apart from other Amish preachers: his fearless preaching on the necessity of holy living, and his frequent travels to preach in other Amish communities. Many Amish bishops and preachers focused heavily on the "Ordnung," or church order (rules), of their community, emphasizing separation from the world by observing strict life and dress codes and by not participating in the surrounding social order more than necessary for daily community life. And this was true of the bishop of our district. We were part of the South District of the Old Order Amish community in Plain City, under the firm hand of our bishop, just two narrow farms away, a two-minute walk down the road. There was palpable tension between Joe Doddy and the bishop, but my protective parents shielded me from it. My father resisted talking about it to his dying day, because "we don't get involved in church controversies," as he put it. This is an example of peace church theology turning inward to the point where "peacemaking" and "peacekeeping" often devolve into avoiding conflict or even any discussion about controversy. My father was not entirely unique in this regard. I have often wondered how our district handled the conflict that I felt but was shielded from in my boyhood. I think my grandfather was something of a spiritual revolutionary, helping to birth a revival movement in our Amish community, sparking major shifts and movements that often caused controversy. You will see below how some of these played out in our extended family.

I have vivid memories of Joe Doddy at work as a preacher: his one armless sleeve would swing back and forth vigorously as he passionately proclaimed the gospel, noting that all of us need to be born again and accept Jesus Christ as our Lord and Savior to gain salvation and eternal life. Church rules might be necessary to keep us separated from the world, but they would not save our souls. Salvation came through faith in Christ alone, which led to transformed living. Joe Doddy was planting the seeds of evangelical faith, including evangelism and missions. The Amish were not supportive of missions while I was growing up. My dad once told me that the Great Commission (Mt. 28: 16-20) was meant only for the twelve Apostles, not for us. (He later changed his mind.) But Joe Doddy was a traveling Amish evangelist, although probably not using that title. A trusted source tells me that this led to many "enemies" within the church opposing his message. I believe it now, although as a child I never thought of him as having enemies. One other distinctive feature that set Joe Doddy and a few other preachers apart: they spoke with dynamic enthusiasm, while many Amish preachers used a more prosaic, dry, almost sing-song style that might lull you to sleep. Enthusiasm seems essential for spreading the Word. (Fun fact:

"enthusiasm" comes from the Greek *en-theos*, "in God," one of Paul's favorite concepts in his New Testament epistles.)

My grandfather went on the road with the message, also bringing return visitors. Other Amish preachers would come to see my grandfather, spend a few days, or even preach guest sermons at our church. Since we lived in the adjoining big house and Grandma Miller ("Joe Mommy") had died when I was quite young, the guest preachers sometimes slept at our house and ate at our table. Thus, I heard many stories from other communities, discovering that life in Pennsylvania, Indiana, or Iowa—even in Amish communities there—could be quite different from our own. As a naturally curious child (my dad said I asked too many questions and compared me to *Yonie Wondernose*, the book sometimes called the "Amish *Curious George*"), I was intrigued by the stories these visiting preachers told. I am sure those stories and my grandfather's travels ignited in me a longing for exploration, discovery, travel, and even missionary activity in faraway lands. This inner stirring helped prepare me for an eventual lifetime of working across cultures, and helped condition me for the many adjustments that would be needed in the years to come as we moved around to various places and cultures at home and abroad.

Mose Doddy (my maternal grandfather) also left a deep impression on me, as he lived on a rented farm with electricity, a telephone, and running water, exposing me to differences within the Amish community, even within my own extended family. This is not the place for a lengthy explanation, but let me note here that the lines between *owning* and *experiencing* modern conveniences were carefully drawn among the Amish, as is still the case in most communities, with local bishops drawing them. So my *maternal* grandfather—and all of us by extension—could *use* the telephone and electricity already installed in his rented farmhouse, since the non-Amish landlord was the *owner* of those worldly conveniences. Outside observers are often mystified by this delineation, as was I in my early years. The easiest way to explain it is to say that all of us who try to follow Jesus' admonition to be *in* but not *of* this world will choose our symbols of separation. The Amish simply draw the line in places different from many others. *Riding* in cars was all right if necessary, but *owning* cars was forbidden. My grandpa also had an old upright Remington typewriter on his roll-top desk, which I was allowed to peck away at endlessly on my visits. I never saw typewriters in any other Amish homes as a little boy. I eventually taught myself to type, as I'm doing at this very moment, likely because of my early pecking away on Grandpa's Remington. Were typewriters also forbidden? I don't know. Maybe Grandpa's landlord (Cephas Atkins, the banker in town) also owned this amazing technology? (For a deeper analysis of Amish culture, see Don Kraybill's wonderful book, *The Riddle of Amish Culture,* Johns Hopkins U Press, 2001)

My frequent visits to Mose Doddy's house, with those wonderful overnight stays, exposed me to the many people from far and near who came and went on a daily basis: Amish neighbors to use the telephone, feed and seed dealers, milk and bread truck drivers, and an endless network of connections that were "normal" for him as a farmer. Also, my Uncle John–Mose Doddy's youngest son and my mother's brother–lived on the adjoining farm with his family, and the two farms were farmed in partnership with my grandfather. Uncle John's family had left the Amish and joined the Mennonites (later, they joined the Baptists), so I would often ride in Uncle John's cars, or on his rubber-tired tractors, use his electric appliances, and even play on that magnificent but forbidden instrument in their living room—a piano! What amazing sounds would emanate from that wondrous box full of secret strings and hammers! I even got to peek inside at times.

Here I need to add a note about music and the Amish. The Amish permitted only plaintive, ancient, Gregorian-chant-style German singing in church, all acapella and in unison (no harmony). Amish youth were allowed to sing a mix of German and English songs during their "singings" (hymn sings), a favorite Sunday-night youth activity approved by the church. Both German and English songs were sung to modern tunes with harmony, so they were often upbeat and lively. The only instrument Amish children and youth were allowed to have was the harmonica, which was considered more of a toy than an instrument. That is why I mastered the harmonica and could play almost anything on it. Years later, I learned to play chords on the guitar and played around on a used accordion I picked up somewhere.

My dad loved to sing. He was often singing and whistling as we worked on the farm. Mom would sing softly as well, or hum along. I fondly remember many of those songs from my childhood. My dad used to play guitar in his youth. I know this because he kept his old guitar upstairs in our spare room until I was old enough to become interested in playing it. That is when he burned it, so he would not become a "bad influence" on his young Amish son. I was devastated, as I loved music and singing, just like my dad. I even heard him play a few chords on Aunt Fran's piano, so I'm guessing maybe he played piano also before he settled down and joined the church. My Grandpa Hostetler had an old phonograph upstairs in his spare room. Sometimes, we grandchildren played with that tempting music machine. I don't know why he kept that vintage wind-up Victrola; I'm sure it was *verboten* by the church. Did his landlord own that also? Maybe I inherited musical genes with my mother's milk and didn't realize it. Forbidden music is like forbidden fruit; the more you forbid it, the more tempting it becomes.

I learned something very valuable from Grandpa Hostetler: he was tolerant and nonjudgmental toward people inside and outside my family who expressed their faith in both Amish and non-Amish ways. (The Amish referred to non-Amish people as "English people," because they used English in daily life and in church, not German or Pennsylvania Dutch, our vernacular language at home.) My many younger Hostetler cousins may not have experienced our grandfather exactly as I did, of course, but these are my images of him. I am sure Uncle John's children have memories different from mine, since they interacted with him daily.

Let me share two of my favorite memories of Mose Doddy. I would sometimes get to travel to town with him in his horse and buggy, and almost always he would take me to the drug store, where we would sit at the old-fashioned marble counter on barstools, sipping huge handmade chocolate milkshakes with cold steam and condensation running down the stainless-steel tumblers. There was no greater joy nor taste in this world! The other special memory came when I was much older, and I asked him one day how he felt about some of the conflicts we were dealing with in the church. He had a profound response, which I never forgot: "I often wonder why we split the church over issues we all agree on ten years later." As a pastor, and later as a Mennonite bishop, I frequently remembered this bit of wisdom from my grandfather. I also remember asking him once how he could live alone for so many years after Grandma had died. He said, "Human beings can adjust to almost anything." Indeed! This wisdom also guided me through the years.

CHAPTER 3

Growing Up on a Farm

Growing up on a farm is fun and hard. Books, postcards, and calendars can make farm life look idyllic and ideal, often evoking collective nostalgia for "the good old days." Folk wisdom suggests that bygone eras of small farms and small towns were mostly peaceful. Life was simpler and less hectic. There were white picket fences everywhere, most days were filled with birds, flowers, and sunny skies with an occasional storm or two. Neighbors helped each other. Children played happily. Most animals were tame and friendly—almost pets. Even traveling in carriages and wagons looks like fun, if you go by the stories and pictures in many of our books.

But this is a very deceptive illusion. Life on the farm could be rough, with plenty of challenges and tragedies to go around. A cursory read of old newspapers will soon supply ample illustrations. Families feuded. Loan sharks and peddlers found ways to get people's money. Big farmers ate up the small farmers. Cities grew and threatened rural communities. Children rebelled and left home. Babies and children died. Winters were hard. Diseases were often rampant. Mother Nature unleashed her fury, often through fire, flood, and storm. Wars threatened and often took the brightest and best young men, sometimes also the horses and the hay. Here is a photo of our farm on the Amish Pike where I was born and raised.

I came into the world right in the middle of World War II, when all 18-year-old men had to register for the draft. This posed a dilemma for Amish and Mennonite young men, along with others in the peace church tradition, all opposed to serving in the military or taking up arms against other humans, even in self-defense. The U.S. government allowed such young men to register as conscientious objectors (to war) and enroll in approved alternative service programs. My Uncle, H. John Hostetler (my mother's youngest brother), did a term of service away from home, perhaps in my father's stead. I remember hearing about young men who served in another's stead when serving away from home was a hardship. As the youngest son, my father had ended up on the home farm, taking up where my grandfather left off, and was the father of a newborn. So, leaving home for him would have presented a hardship for the family. Uncle John, single and still living at home, could more easily get away for a few years. He ended up working at several Civil Public Service (CPS) camps, eventually in Luray, VA, along with other young men from Anabaptist or other backgrounds. It occurs to me now that this exposure to other cultures and communities might help explain why he was the only one of my mother's siblings to leave the Amish church. Who knows?

As the firstborn son, I inherited a lot of responsibility as I helped my parents get established in parenting and farming. My father had hurt his back in a fall from the silo, and my grandfather—while still living on the farm but handicapped after losing one arm—shifted the burden of running the home place onto my dad's shoulders. I helped raise my five siblings, especially the older ones. This went without saying in most Amish families. Families were large. The older children helped raise the younger ones. Even in school, teachers relied on older students to help teach younger students, especially in one-room schools. I was given major responsibilities around the house and barn, helping mom and dad with all the hard farm work without electricity and other modern conveniences.

A typical day at our house began at 5:00 a.m. Mom and Dad would get up, start the fire, and light the gas lamps and lanterns. Soon, they would get us older ones out of bed to help with morning chores before getting ready for school. Dad and I would take several lanterns to the chicken house and barn, waking up the animals in the process. There were chickens to feed, cows to milk, and hogs to slop. Winter mornings were cold and hard. Often, we would find a sick calf or colt that needed attention and medicine. Perhaps after breakfast, Dad would need to get on his bike or buggy and go to Grandpa Hostetler's house to call the vet. Some of the young chicks might have wandered too far from the warm heater overnight and died in the cold. They would be collected and disposed of in the landfill behind the barn. Milk had to be taken to the milk house and kept cold in shiny metal cans for the milk truck to pick up later. Our milk went to the local cheese house, where it was made into Swiss cheese. Sometimes cows developed mastitis, and their milk had to be discarded until the cow could be medicated back to health. Milking by hand was usually a warm experience, since the cows were close together in the cow barn and we sat on low stools between their warm bodies. But there was always the strong scent of manure mixing with the milk, along with the mewing of cats begging for a squirt of warm milk shot in their direction. Floors were powdered with lime to make them less slippery, but our boots and coats still smelled like the cow barn when we went into the house for breakfast at 7:00, ready for a hearty farmers' breakfast.

By then, Mom would have the lunches packed and all our school clothes laid out ready to wear, and a hot steaming table full of eggs, toast, bacon or sausage, and perhaps oatmeal or cold cereal. There wasn't much time to eat all this, as we had to rush and get ready for school. Most Amish kids rode a school bus to the Amish school, but since Plainview School was on a corner of our farm, my siblings and I just walked a few hundred feet down the road and we were there! Of course, we had no excuse for being late, even on snowy days. Grandpa Joe Doddy would have been to the school early, firing up the coal furnace and making sure the building was nice and warm when we got there. As the school janitor, he was a familiar grandfatherly presence, chatting with the students during the day, and leaving his famous drawings of birds and animals on the blackboards in the three classrooms. Sometimes he would add a Bible verse. So for a day or two, the teacher would mark off that corner of the board to be saved and savored before erasing it for regular classroom use.

Even though Joe Doddy was missing his left arm, he had a metal hook and leather halter attached to his left stub and managed to do just about anything other men did with two arms and hands. My grandmother often said that he got more done with one arm than many other men with two! Of course, as humble Amish farmer folk, we were not supposed to brag, but I suppose my grandma could be forgiven for this little comeback whenever others expressed sympathy for Joe Doddy's unfortunate handicap. Subconsciously, it also reinforced the unspoken work ethic, which held that everyone in the community has something to contribute to the common good, regardless of age or disability. Children with special needs were accepted and praised for their achievements. An interesting side note: most "normal" children were seldom praised for their hard work—hard work was assumed for all regular community members. Praising children for their achievements would be too likely to engender pride and competition. The less fortunate, however, could be commended as an expression of empathy.

School life (here's a grainy shot of me as a school boy) will be explored more fully in the next chapter, but let me add a few more details about Amish farm life, as I remember it. All of us worked hard, as there were hundreds of daily tasks necessary for successful farming.

In general, you could say Dad was in charge of the barn and the fields, while Mom was in charge of the house, garden, and yard. But that is a deceptive oversimplification, as Mom and my sisters helped with barn and field work as needed. We boys and Dad often helped with chores in the house and garden as well. We were in many ways "one big happy family" as we sang, worked, talked, played, and sometimes squabbled, as we shared the multitude of duties on the farm. I have many fond memories of helping my Mom with the laundry on Mondays. There were huge iron kettles over a furnace in the wash house, where I helped build a fire and bring the water to a boil. I helped make sure the Maytag washer was working. The engine needed constant refueling with gas and oil, belts and pulleys needed to be lubricated, and the wringer rollers needed to be cleaned. Then there were the outdoor washlines to be stretched and wiped clean before hanging up long lines of wet, clean clothes. In the wintertime, these often froze on the line, but no matter. When the sun came out later, they dried and smelled so fresh! It was a joy to run back into the warm wash house and defrost my nose and toes before taking out a new basket of wet clothes to hang on the line.

Because we did many loads of soiled and sweaty farm clothes, the water had to be changed often. The furnace was kept stoked for several hours to keep plenty of hot water ready until the weekly ritual was over. The water was pumped by hand into the huge kettles, so the kettles had to be kept full, then emptied, cleaned, and covered until next week. One very fond memory I have is a joke Mom and I passed along for years: I read somewhere in a magazine that many people washed their clothes in "lukewarm mud," not keeping the water in the washing machine hot enough. So every once in a while, Mom would tell me to stick my hands into her "lukewarm mud," to remind me that she always had her laundry water piping hot! Precious memories! Mom and I had a lot of fun working together, joking, laughing, singing, and playing little pranks on each other. My mother worked harder and longer hours than anyone else I knew, but I remember those early days as happy and full of fun, despite all the hard work. Mom and I were good friends. She was short, and I was tall, so in my teen years, when we would go to town together for the weekly grocery shopping, she was often mistaken for my sister. She did look very youthful for much of her life. And as her oldest, I got to do things with her that many boys did not—baking, cleaning, scrubbing walls and windows, washing dishes, helping bathe the little ones, and so on.

Dad and I had fun, too, but I remember him as a rather strict new father in my early years. We worked together on the farm—along with my grandfather—on everything from planting to harvesting. There was always plenty to do, as farming is the kind of work that is never finished. By the time the plowing was done, it was time to prepare for planting. When the crops were planted, it was time to get the machinery and barn ready for harvesting, after the weeding and cultivating were done, of course. And there were always the animals to care for. Fence rows needed cleaning and trimming. There was barn cleaning, manure hauling, and machinery maintenance, building painting, seed and fertilizer purchasing, and on and on. Baby animals grew and had to be taken to market. Horses needed to be fed and groomed daily. Needless to say, farming is a complicated business. To balance all the life cycles with the yearly weather patterns was not something you could simply wake up one morning and begin doing. It came from generations of observing and learning in families and communities; it always needed to be adapted for each locale and climate. Farmers were forever sharing stories, ideas, newspaper and magazine articles, and the newest products on the market, from seed to fertilizer to tractors and farm machines or tools. Anyone who thinks farming is easy and always the same obviously has not farmed very long at all. Someone once quipped, "Marriage is like farming; you have to start over every morning." There is much wisdom in that kernel of truth.

My earliest memories of helping Dad around the house and barn involved fixing things. My father could fix anything! When I say fix, I mean repair or improve. He was an entrepreneur at heart, always reading about new inventions or coming up with his own. There was always room for improvement. I loved holding a wrench or screwdriver and shining a flashlight under the oven, washing machine, or tractor while Dad figured out which parts needed replacing, tightening, or improving. Learning how to fix things is part of growing up on a farm. Every farmer had a workshop with an array of interesting tools hanging above the workbench. Many had welders, grinders, drills, saws, and overflowing toolboxes so that they could have started a store or a furniture business. My insatiable curiosity must have come from my father, though he sometimes complained that I was too curious and didn't need to poke my nose into everything. A very early memory has me climbing under the stove alongside my dad, getting in his way until he said, "Sonny, you take the cake!" (My boyhood nickname was Sonny.)

My father was a very kind and loving man, even though he was quite strict at first. My hunch is that the first child always gets the strictest rules until the parents get enough experience to realize that no one is perfect—not even parents—and that no two children are alike. That the same discipline may not work at all with another sibling, even if that sibling were a twin. That we all learn from our mistakes. That children will learn more by what they live than by what they are told. Dad loved people, loved life, and loved to sing. I can still remember and sing many of those early songs he sang as we worked. Some were serious hymns—English or German—while others were silly or just plain fun. Mom also sang, but I mostly remember her humming or whistling while she worked. I picked up a lot of my worldview-shaping theology by pondering the songs we sang or reflecting on the scriptures we memorized. One of my dad's favorite songs was, "This world is not my home/I'm just a-passing through/My treasures are laid up, somewhere beyond the blue ." I find myself singing this song more and more as I get older.

Since the Amish forbade photographs of people (based on the biblical command not to make graven images), our walls were covered with decorative plaques highlighting Bible verses or wise sayings. One favorite was, "Only one life, 'twill soon be past/Only what's done for Christ will last."

You could say there was much "Wisdom Literature" hanging on the walls of Amish homes, mostly in English. That helped us children internalize Bible truths we could not always grasp from the German sermons at church. That was also good for me as a curious lad who liked to ask too many questions (my dad and the preachers would agree), since the Amish in my community were not prone to discussing their theology. Questions we raised as kids were often met with the rejoinder, "You're too young" or "You'll understand when you get older." Amish life is more caught than taught. As is true in any culture, you learn by observing and doing. You may get answers later; more likely, you will not. Like my mom liked to say, "We've just always done it this way." A favorite reply of any Amish parent when children's questions piled up was simply, "We've got work to do."

This can be discouraging to any young person pondering life's many inconsistencies and trying to bring a unified worldview into focus. For example, I often wondered why our houses had to be white, while buggies (and later cars) had to be black, but our tractors could be any wild, modern color that came along. Or why we could use all kinds of wheeled vehicles, but the wheels had to be made of steel, not rubber. Later, we could have rubber wheels, only if bolted to steel rims. My father and I spent most of one spring cutting up rubber tires for our Ford tractor and bolting them onto hard steel rims. Outsiders looking in offered all kinds of explanations ("It's because the devil rules the air."). But those weren't the answers we got growing up. Often we got no answers, or I got answers, but those might be different from my cousin Johnny's answers from his father. Perhaps if our tires had air in them, we would use our tractors too much for running around on the road, almost like cars or trucks. But the airless tires made road travel rather easy anyway, so that answer really didn't always work. Using tractors only for field work was a hard rule to follow.

I learned to lift and carry quite heavy loads at an early age. Our cattle feed came in 100-pound burlap bags, and we often slung them on our shoulders and carried them to the feeding trough or storage area. Fertilizer came in 80-pound bags. Hauling manure was hard work, and manure is heavy to lift with a fork. Later, we actually got a manure loader for the front of our tractor, and that was a huge improvement! At first, we put up loose hay upstairs in the barn, in the haymow, which was not very heavy but simply hard to handle, dusty, and itchy, as dust filtered in around one's collar or pant legs. Later on, when we baled our hay, it was easier to handle, but the bales are quite heavy. Again, Amish children learn early to lift and carry heavy loads, which, no doubt, contributes to the traditional slouching posture while sitting or walking. Subconsciously, this was a cultural value as well: if you sat, stood, or walked too upright, you might be thought haughty or proud, putting yourself "above" others.

My grandfather also kept his horse and perhaps a few other animals in our barn, so I often found him there while I was doing my chores. I remember one painful lesson I learned from him while feeding the horses. I kept calling out, "Doddy! Doddy!" and he would say, "What?" "Oh, nothing," I replied (in Pennsylvania Dutch, of course). I thought this game amusing, until after about the third time he said, "Sonny, listen! Don't do that! Sometimes you may call and really need me, but I won't answer because I'll think you are playing." As you can see, I never forgot that lesson.

Later on, after we began using tractors as well as horses, I remember trying to read a book or learn a new song on the tractor while plowing a straight furrow, only to see with a backward glance that I had gone crooked and the plow was choked up with weeds and dirt. How could I quickly undo all that and try not to leave a trace so Dad wouldn't know? All in all, successful farming brings a deep satisfaction, knowing that God put us here to be "keepers of the garden," as he told Adam and Eve; to till the soil and become an integral part of the cycle of "seed-time and harvest" as long as the earth shall endure. It was all very much like being part of a symphony, sometimes conducting, sometimes playing an instrument. The music of the spheres. Birds and animals, plants and butterflies, humans and insects, all singing the song of the Master Composer. Hallelujah!

Here's a photo of Dad and Mom relaxing at home.

CHAPTER 4

Plainview School Days

The new Amish-Mennonite school in Plain City opened in the middle of the school year, on December 8, 1947–a few weeks before Christmas–because the new building was not finished in time for the beginning of the school year. The 67 inaugural students, grades 1 - 10, thus began their time at the new school in the middle of the academic year. The next year a third classroom was added, and 106 students began the first full year at the new school, Plainview Christian School, built on land donated by my grandfather on a corner of our farm.

I was part of the first grade for that first full year, 1948-1949, and completed all ten grades at Plainview. There were eight in my class. Our teacher was Virginia Weaver ("Miss Virginia"), a college-educated Mennonite who was hired as one of the three teachers that year, all three of whom were college-educated, certified, and brought in from other Mennonite communities. I mention this because later the school would hire teachers from the local Amish-Mennonite community who were not certified and who had no college background (including me!). Why the school board initially wanted certified teachers but later allowed that policy to lapse is complicated. In his history of the school, Enos Stutzman offers a few hints. He writes: "'Little Jonas' [Gingerich] made many a call to look for teachers. In compliance with the standards set by state officials [State of Ohio officials with whom the school board had met before opening the school], they sought certified teachers. They were finally successful in locating two young Mennonite ladies who fit the bill, Gladys Brunk . . . and Goldie Weaver."

His records indicate that several more certified Mennonite teachers were brought in from elsewhere for several more years, but as time went on more teachers were hired from within the local community, as it became more difficult and expensive to find enough certified teachers.

He also mentions that some Amish parents became worried that the Mennonite teachers, who taught Bible classes and Bible memory, were having too much influence at the school, which they feared would erode Amish customs. In Chapter 2 Stutzman explains that the influence of Mennonite teachers, along with visiting Mennonite evangelists holding revival meetings in the local Mennonite churches, did indeed stir a new sense of Christian commitment among the older students. Some of the more "orthodox" among the Amish began to move to other Amish communities, a trend that continued for many years. Today, there are no Old Order Amish churches left in the Plain City community; only Beachy Amish or various Mennonite branches remain. (For more details, see *A History of Plainview Christian School*, by Enos D. Stutzman. Prairie View Press, Neche, ND, 2020)

As mentioned earlier, I was always a curious child. I wanted to know how everything worked, how to fix things, and even how to invent new toys, like the toy hay baler we constructed from items found in Dad's shop. So school sounded like an adventure to me, and I was excited to finally be able to go. They tell me I walked around the new school that first week holding hands with my cousin Louise, also in first grade, who lived a few farms away and whom I knew well from playing with my cousins. Apparently, I was a happy camper.

Miss Virginia was a wonderful teacher. She took a keen interest in her young Amish pupils and instilled in us a deep love for God, the Bible, and each other. She was a beautiful soul with a tender spirit, a prayerful and thoughtful demeanor not always evident in our Amish community. As she taught us the ABC's, numbers, handwriting (printing and cursive), phonics, music, and art, along with creative play at recess and lunch, she did so with a sense that learning was important. I relished all this. I will be forever grateful to Miss Virginia for giving me this incredible educational foundation, launching me into a lifetime of learning, a desire to explore all of God's infinite creation, and a desire to share all new discoveries with those around me.

Teachers have a major influence on all our lives, for good or for ill. The best teachers, no matter what their subject, instill an excitement for learning, an awe for discovery. At least that has been my experience, from first grade through grad school. Every subject, even the most mundane, becomes exciting if the teacher is excited about it. Wouldn't you agree? I had many fine teachers at Plainview, but two stand out especially for me, Virginia Weaver (grades 1 and 2) and Esther Hilty (grades 6 and 8), perhaps because they were Mennonite women who wore colorful print dresses (not allowed among the Amish), with an education and a professional bearing different from most Amish women I knew. They exhibited a different way of being in the world, a world much bigger than the Amish world I grew up in. I will say more about Esther Hilty later, as her influence on my development was inestimable.

A typical day at Plainview would begin with a devotional, prayer, and singing. This opening activity included the entire classroom. Then the academic classes began. Since there were several grade levels in each of the three classrooms, the teacher would try to use a low voice while teaching English, say, to grade 1 in the first row, but the students in the other grades in the other rows would inevitably hear a lot of the lesson, even if they were doing their own assignments. This could be seen as a distraction or an advantage. Of course, the teacher would have to keep an eye on the whole room, even while teaching only one subject to one row, maintaining order throughout. While this may sound chaotic to an outside observer, it soon became a familiar routine and worked rather well. Older students who were ahead in their work could help some of the younger ones who needed "tutoring."

The school had no electricity, telephone, running water, or indoor plumbing in the early days. Two outhouses in opposite corners of the school yard served our purposes, rain or shine! They were far enough away to prevent aromatic intrusion into the classrooms, even with the window open on hot days. The coal-fired furnace in the basement heated the whole school without electric blowers. Some days were chilly, and we had to wear coats even in class. Joe Doddy, my grandfather living in the Doddy Haus next to us, was the janitor, and he always fired up the furnace early every morning to make sure the classrooms were warm by the time students arrived. There were large windows that let in plenty of light, but on the coldest, darkest days, camping lanterns were lit and suspended from hooks to provide enough light to study by.

Every morning, I would get up around 5:00, help with morning farm chores–feeding the chickens, gathering eggs, slopping the hogs, and milking the cows–or help Mom in the kitchen, eat breakfast, get dressed for school, then walk the 1,000 feet along the road to the school. I usually carried a packed lunch to eat with my friends, though sometimes I would walk home if needed. Living this close to the school meant my parents were often called on to help if something broke, if one of the students got hurt, or especially if someone tore a shirt or pants during recess, and Mom would have to stitch it back together temporarily. This created many laughs and lasting memories. If you tore your pants during a softball game, everyone at school found out immediately, and that evening, most families heard the story at the supper table.

School was a big adjustment for those of us who came from Amish homes. At home we spoke Pennsylvania Dutch, and at church all the singing, praying, and preaching were done in high German, much of which we children didn't understand. In school, however, we had to learn how to read and speak proper English. Our Mennonite teachers did not know our mother tongue, so we had to learn English. We were discouraged from speaking Pennsylvania Dutch at school. Of course, we could always whisper to each other in our mother tongue if we wanted to put one over on the teacher.

Singing in English was revolutionary! We learned how to read the words and the music, sometimes singing in rounds and even clapping to nursery rhyme tunes. Our teachers taught us how to harmonize. Amazing! This was something we could get into and enjoy, far different from the plaintive, slow, German dirge-like unison chants at church, which seemed endless and meaningless. Memorizing Bible verses and poems cemented the new and living language into our memory banks. Learning was fun. Art and music sparked our creative imaginations. In middle school, my friends and I even began writing short stories and formed a secret book club.

We called it the Book Worm Club (BWC), but to keep it secret, we reversed the initials to CWB. If anyone asked us what that stood for, it stood for Crazy Woman's Baby. I still have a dozen or so hand-written stories in my box of treasures. Sadly, they never got published, which is just as well. They were not particularly noteworthy. But they represented the new world of reading being opened to us Amish kids.

The well-ordered school days took some getting used to, as life on the farm can be rather flexible and free-flowing, depending on the season and the weather. When the morning bell rang, we took our seats, and structured learning began. We sat up straight, paid attention to the teacher, and raised our hands to ask or answer a question. We had one recess mid-morning, then had more lessons until noon. Lunch was a special time. We would sit in clusters out on the lawn, on the playground, in the basement, or even in our classroom. It was a time for chatting with friends, trading lunches, telling jokes, and playing games—all in Pennsylvania Dutch, of course. When the weather was nice, those were wonderful times.

After lunch, especially in the younger grades, we would have "story time" when the teacher would read from a book to the whole room while we put our heads down on our desks to listen (or nap!), a clever way to settle down our restless minds, ready to get back to work. Sometimes they read short stories, sometimes a chapter at a time from a children's book or a book of missionary stories. This opened up the wonderful world of books for all of us. After more lessons and a short mid-afternoon recess, the yellow bus would arrive at 4:00 p.m., and we would head for home. Of course, I could get home before all my friends, since I only had to walk a few steps or even hop over the fence, and I was home! After a snack, homework or free time, it was time to do evening chores and get ready for dinner (supper, as we called it), and evening activities.

I have many wonderful memories from my ten years at this new school. I will only highlight a few here. Some not-so-pleasant memories need not be included in this account.

I remember how we loved to sing from the little red songbook for children: folk songs, nursery rhymes, songs teaching simple Bible truths, and lessons for life. We also played games that made recess and lunch times fun and taught us cooperation and good sportsmanship. I especially remember the many Friday afternoons when classes dismissed early, and the entire school went outside to play softball. Many students, both boys and girls, became very good at softball because it was the main sport allowed by the Amish. We also played some basketball and flag football, but softball was king! Of course, there were always tag, hide-and-seek, and other games that most of us enjoyed.

As we moved into the middle and upper grades, we learned to read music, keep time (conduct group singing), harmonize, and even perform solos. I remember distinctly how Esther Hilty taught us to read music. She stunned us by saying if we could learn to read music, we could sing all the way through the hymnal–even songs we had never heard before. Indeed, she led us as we sang all the way through the blue *Church Hymnal,* the Mennonite hymnal in use at that time. That was an exhilarating experience that ignited a love of singing in us. She put us into groups to sing duets, trios, quartets, and choruses (choirs) for special occasions such as the Christmas program or the closing ceremonies at the end-of-year picnic. Of course, it was all a cappella singing because we were not allowed to use instruments. Sometimes, when singing a solo, we discovered musical talents we didn't know we had. The music she taught us spilled over later into youth groups and choirs at our various churches. Music united us and built up our faith, instilling moral and theological values.

Miss Hilty and other teachers also brought the Bible to life through morning devotionals and Bible courses. They challenged us to have a living relationship with Jesus as our Savior and Lord. They led in spontaneous prayers and even asked us to pray. The Amish read most of their prayers from German prayer books or memorize prayers such as the Lord's Prayer. We learned to pray about everyday life and talk to God just like we talk to a friend. That was refreshingly liberating and made prayer a part of daily living, not just a ceremonial ritual for special occasions. We learned that faith is loving God and our neighbor with all our heart, a daily walk with God, guided by the Holy Spirit within us.

These Mennonite teachers modeled a simple faith, expressed in joyful love for others. They brought a certain decorum, a humble professionalism, and dignity that drew us to them. We were more used to a rough-and-tumble, down-on-the-farm earthiness of the Amish culture. This new level of refinement took some getting used to, but it was somewhat contagious as well. We learned a new level of respect, of kindness in dealing with others, and new ways of problem-solving. The Bible teaching and spiritual singing they taught us brought deep spiritual stirrings within some of us. Convictions grew until we wanted to confess our sins and confess Jesus as our Savior and Lord. They led us in simple prayers, and we rejoiced in a new and living faith, which we shared with each other but didn't know how to share with our parents.

We came from homes and churches where faith was something you gradually grew into over time, not an instantaneous experience of being "born again." Many of our parents would not understand nor necessarily approve, but how could they object to our new attitudes, our readiness to listen and obey? A revival movement spread through the Plain City community, causing some of the more "orthodox" Amish families to move away, and many others to join more "progressive" churches. Enos Stutzman's history of Plainview traces the historical outlines of this transformation. Of course, not all were drawn to these new ideas.

Some outright resistance from students and parents was inevitable and showed up from time to time in various ways.

Plainview had its share of troublemakers from the beginning. Some students did not like school and were not really interested in learning. The Amish misgivings about education in general did not help. Every teacher at Plainview had to learn to maintain control of their classroom, some more successfully than others. Students sometimes whispered among themselves, passed notes, shot paper wads at each other or at the teacher, taped unpleasant surprises to the teacher's chair or hid them in her desk drawers, carved initials into their desks, pulled girls' hair, and pulled other typical pranks. Students were sometimes late, absent, or refused to turn in homework. Unruly behavior and outright disobedience were not uncommon.

One vivid memory I distinctly recall involved a race at lunch time. A group of us were eating our lunch out by the roadside, sitting on the slope of the ditch by the driveway. After we finished eating, some of the older boys challenged us to a race. They got several of us to run a specified distance from driveway to driveway. The promised prize was a piece of chocolate candy. I won, to rousing cheers, and gladly ate the chocolate only to learn that it was not candy at all, but Ex-Lax, a chocolate-flavored laxative! No! Not fair. I went inside and pulled Miss Hilty aside, explained my predicament and wondered what I should do. She was unfazed and told me to walk home, ask my mom for nutmeg and a spoon. I brought them back to the school, took a teaspoon of nutmeg washed down with water and nothing ever happened. As you can see, Miss Hilty had a lot of practical wisdom in addition to all her classroom knowledge.

Two highlights of every school year were the Christmas program and the end-of-school picnic. The Christmas program was a big production every year, taking weeks of preparation. The centerpiece was always a reenactment of the nativity story, with all grade levels participating. Every year, there were tryouts for the roles of Mary, Joseph, angels, shepherds, wise men, and narrator. Costumes were made, sets were designed, scripts were written, and rehearsals were planned. Between acts in the play various groups would sing Christmas carols. The younger grades would sing as a group. Older students sang in trios, quartets, or even solos. As a grand finale, the entire student body would get on stage as a combined choir to present rousing renditions of Christmas classics. Christmas was the one time we were allowed to do drama, to put on a live play, and have special music, without instruments, of course. Because it told the story of Jesus's birth, the Amish approved. Normally, dramatic performances were off limits. It was the one time we Amish students got to act and sing in front of a live audience, a rarity in our community. It was actually good training for public speaking, acting, and singing.

The school picnic at the end of each year was also a big event, but without the pageantry and drama. Since we had only ten grades, there was no actual "graduation" from the school. Everyone simply passed or failed, and the departing tenth-graders received certificates of completion. It was a low-key ending to the school year. Usually, there was a short program: the principal or someone else gave an encouraging speech, report cards were handed out, and a prayer of blessing was offered for everyone at the school. Then we had a huge picnic, really a community potluck meal, followed by softball. Usually the older boys played against the men, most of them parents, in the first game. After that, several more impromptu softball games would be played. People lingered throughout the afternoon to watch, share stories, laugh, and get ready for a summer off to work on the farm, enjoy family reunions, or take short vacation trips.

Even though Plainview School did not meet state academic standards, it provided a solid Anabaptist grounding in the faith, with sufficient basic knowledge for living a useful life in this world. The Mennonite teachers, brought in from other communities, modeled a vibrant Christian life that emphasized holy living, sharing one's faith, and a level of decency and respect that was not always evident in the Amish culture. The school became a change agent, a vital part of the spiritual revival sweeping through the Plain City community, a revival that caused many of the more "orthodox" among the Amish to move away for fear they would lose their Amish ways.

I often look back on my days at Plainview, first as a student and then as a teacher, and realize how seminal that school was in shaping my character and life. I am forever grateful to my grandfather and all the others who first had the vision for a new school in our community. I believe most of my classmates would agree.

CHAPTER 5

Sudden Turn to Teaching

After I "graduated" from Grade 10–the norm for Amish kids at Plainview School–I worked for one year on the farm with my dad. I also worked part-time as a carpenter for Ora Gingerich, as did many other Amish boys after finishing school. It was a great way to earn a little money, experience getting a paycheck, and learn marketable skills. Ora (or "Orrie," as we called him) was an Amish contractor who built most of the new buildings in the Plain City Amish community. He and his crew also built many of the new split-level houses in Columbus's suburbs. My dad, who sometimes also worked for Orrie, taught me a lot about carpentry and handyman repairs, and like most farm kids, I picked up many lifetime skills just by growing up on a farm.

But now I could learn from Orrie, a brilliant professional builder. I learned how to do carpentry work, from laying the foundation for a house to finishing the walls and windows. We built everything from farm structures to fancy suburban houses. Working for Orrie gave me exposure to worlds hitherto unknown to me. I met many people outside the Amish world in the Columbus area as our crew interacted with neighboring crews, owners, and businesspeople who delivered building products or services (electricity, water, gas), signed contracts, and enforced city building codes, etc. For this sheltered Amish farm boy, life suddenly became an adventure every day. We would be picked up early by Ray Stutzman or other crew members with cars. Ora and his brother Dan, who ran the crews, were both Old Order Amish and thus could not own or operate cars. They usually employed several Mennonite or unbaptized Amish young men with cars who could thus drive the crews to and from work as part of their contract. Ray usually picked us up around 6:00 in the morning–rain or shine, snow, sleet, or ice–5 or 6 days a week. We would start at 7:00 and work until 5:30, with a 30-minute lunch break, routinely putting in 10-hour days. We worked hard but had lots of fun as well. It was great training for the world of work, with a generous amount of church talk, theology, and world views thrown in over lunch or on the drive to and from work. It was an exhausting, challenging, and exhilarating change from farm life.

It would not be far wrong to claim that almost every young man in the PC Amish community at some time or other "worked for Orrie." In fact, to this day, many of my peers and their sons can evoke instant grins and chuckles by the mere mention of "working for Orrie." It will usually be followed by, "Do you remember the time when . . .?" And the stories begin. Stories of getting stuck in the snow, of accidents and broken bones, of going to work in zero-degree, near-blizzard weather when no other builders were at work, and of wondering how Ora always stayed two steps ahead of the weather, the owners, and the crews. He would usually have his work planned so well that on nice days, we did outdoor work, and during inclement weather, we did indoor work. He usually had numerous jobs going on at once, so we usually had work, even when others were laid off. Ora was truly an Amish entrepreneur and a savvy businessman, even while conscientiously living within the "Ordnung" (Amish church rules). He would often walk across the field in the pre-dawn hours to use his neighbor's phone, check the weather, and arrange work sites for the day.

As I was getting used to this new combination of farming and carpentry, only one short year after finishing 10th grade at Plainview, I got a call that would change my life forever. The Plainview school board came calling. They had a dilemma: the new high school teacher they had just hired could not arrive in time for the start of the new school year. He still had some college coursework to finish and would not be able to come until close to Thanksgiving. Would I consider standing in as a substitute for him, teaching grades six through ten until he arrived?

This unexpected turn of events left me speechless. Why me? Why not someone with some teaching or leadership experience? Apparently, they were desperate. Had they exhausted all other options? Why not a school board member? This would require some serious prayer and discussion, which my parents and I promised to do.

How could I, a 17-year-old who had just finished the very materials I was now being asked to teach, even consider such a task? Could I control a classroom full of students only a few years younger than I was? Like most other Amish boys, I was on a path to farming and carpentry, following in the steps of my father and grandfather. That's what Amish boys grew up to be, generation after generation. To think outside that box was rare. Suddenly, unexpectedly, I was given not only the opportunity, but the mandate, to think outside that box. On the one hand, I was honored and humbled that the board would even consider hiring me. Apparently, they considered me capable, or they would not have asked. On the other hand, they were asking me to teach the very students who were my "classmates" only a year ago, including some of my siblings and cousins. We had five grades together in one room, so even though we were in different grades, we felt like classmates because we were all learning together in one classroom, taught by one teacher.

No teenager I know would be too quick to say yes to such an invitation. The pranks, the gossip, the antics of school children, the cut-ups in every classroom, the taunting of the teacher, or the deliberate defiance of the rules–all of these realities raced through my mind as I discussed the request with my parents. There was not much time to consider all the pros and cons, as school would start in a few weeks, and the board needed a temporary substitute–NOW!

After prayerful consideration, my parents and I decided I could probably handle the teaching position for at least a month or so, until the professional, college-trained new teacher arrived, and then my life could return to "normal." So we said yes, and suddenly I was the new Interim Principal and High School Teacher at Plainview Christian Day School. That felt strange, and I plunged into serious preparation. I knew all of the courses to be taught, having just taken them myself. I had kept most of my notebooks and tests. The textbooks were the same ones kept at the school and used year after year until they were tattered and had to be replaced. I knew all the students and families at the school, as well as the other current teacher. Having spent ten years at the Amish/Mennonite school my parents, grandparents, and others in our community founded, I knew most of the ins and outs and would need no orientation. I only needed to change roles from student to teacher, and I hoped the students would accept it.

School started a week or two before my 18th birthday, so technically, I began teaching school at age 17. Those first few weeks of school are now a blur, but I remember it felt surreal. My life had taken a sudden turn that I could never have imagined. How could I go from being an Amish farm kid–without a high school diploma–to dressing professionally (not really an Amish category), and standing every day in front of grades 6,7,8,9, and 10, teaching every subject from English to math to Bible to biology? I know I prayed mightily for daily grace and leaned heavily on the school board to back up my authority as a teacher and principal.

It felt very strange when the county superintendent of schools would show up occasionally for a brief visit to make sure things were going well. Looking back, I am amazed that the local authorities allowed the Amish to have their own schools and hire inexperienced teachers. I remember with great fondness some of the "professional" traits I picked up from Rolla Webster, the county superintendent, such as carrying crisp white index cards in one's shirt pocket next to a shiny, bright fountain pen, for example. One never knows when one might need to write a note or a reminder to oneself or someone else; this way, you're always prepared! I have worn out many fountain pens and thousands of index cards in my life. Throughout my years as a teacher and church leader, I never felt fully dressed and ready for the day without my cards and pen in my pocket. I admired Mr. Webster's genuine humility in his professional standing and his respect for everyone he worked with, from the

Amish farmer to the governor of Ohio. I stayed in touch with him for many years and was genuinely saddened when I learned of his death.

I know that being friends with the Madison County Superintendent of Schools did much to prepare me for a lifetime of professional teaching and relating to a wide variety of people. As noted above, working on Ora's carpentry crew in the suburbs of Columbus also helped prepare me to interact daily with the outside world (the "English" people, as the Amish would say). Ora was Old Order Amish, and he built many "Amish" buildings in the local community, but he also built some of the most expensive split-level suburban homes in Upper Arlington, the most affluent suburb of Columbus. Ironically, years later, I did my OSU student teaching at Upper Arlington High School, and already felt partially "at home" because of Ora. I was always bewildered by the fact that we lived in plain houses with no phones or electricity, yet we built some of the nicest suburban houses in the region, whose finished basements often had full bars and game rooms, with cabinets from local Amish cabinet shops! Don't try too hard to make all things Amish fit into a neat, logical system; you will only get frustrated! (As I mentioned earlier, Kraybill's brilliant *The Riddle of Amish Culture* will help you make sense of all this.)

Even though those first few months of teaching are now a blur, let me pull up a few memories. I know that the students tried to take advantage of me as an inexperienced teacher. They tested every teacher who ever taught at Plainview, so I knew from experience to be prepared–and I also knew from experience who the likely perpetrators would be. I know that the school board heavily reinforced my status from day one, since they knew this experiment could potentially be a disaster. I had unconditional support from them, my parents, and my grandfather, who came every morning to stoke the furnace. Our home farm and family were only a few hundred feet away in case I needed them for backup. I imagine the students must have been afraid to act up that fall. Looking back, I realize that the parents and school board had a vested interest in my success, as they needed the school year to start on time (earlier than the public schools) so that it could also end on time (early) and their children would be available to help at home.

In any case, things went surprisingly well. I would begin each day with devotional meditations from the Bible, lead singing, and prepare all of us for a day of diligent study. We had regular classes for all five grades, and since all the students were in one large classroom, they could "listen in" on all the subjects, even though I tried to lower my voice and talk only to the grade level in question. The smarter students in the younger grades were able to learn much of the subject matter of the higher grades before they actually got there. Also, those advanced students in the upper grades could help those students struggling in the lower grades. It was all a beautiful extension of the Amish concept of community.

The daily routine included all the usual academic subjects, such as English, math, history, along with morning recess, lunch, afternoon recess, and art and music. We sang together as a class, and we also had a choir ("chorus") that sang at special occasions. Friday afternoons were a weekly highlight, as we would dismiss early for the last few periods of the day, spent outside playing softball and other games, or for a variety of indoor games and contests if the weather was bad. Amish youth are some of the best softball players you will find anywhere, because it was the one sport where we were allowed serious competition along with full participation by all, girls included. This weekly routine was a rare and effective combination for community building. I fondly remember many lunchtimes when I challenged my students to chess games (I was self-taught), and many of them were able to beat me. That meant success. I helped keep the school newspaper going (we renamed it *The Plainview Compeer*), which featured many of their stories and artwork. We established a great rapport, and this was beginning to be fun.

But the new teacher was scheduled to arrive later in the fall, which he did, and I, somewhat reluctantly, I believe, went back to farming and carpentry about a month or so before Christmas.

I was not prepared for what happened next: the new teacher was not very familiar with the local Pennsylvania Dutch Amish culture, so the students gave him a very rough time. Even though he had a college education, international missionary experience, and the professional bearing of a learned man, he seemed like an outsider, representing the "English" or non-Amish world, which the Amish students found hard to respect. (This is a broad-brush-stroke portrayal and not completely fair, as he brought many fine qualities and resources to the school as well, but for the next part of my story, this portrayal seems necessary.) It got so bad that the school board came to ask my parents and me whether I would consider returning after Christmas and continuing to teach.

Well, this was awkward! They said they would keep the new teacher but add me to the mix, which meant we now had three teachers at the school. Furthermore, they would divide the school so that grades 1 - 4 would remain with their current teacher; grades 5 - 7 would be taught by the new college-grad teacher; I would teach grades 8 - 10, now a "quasi high school", which we would move to the small, vacant one-room Oak Grove School a few miles away. This was radical! This was Amish creative restructuring at work, to fit emerging realities. Needless to say, the 1959-60 academic year at Plainview was an unexpected adventure for me and for everyone concerned. After Christmas, I settled into the serious business of becoming a real educator. The pre-Christmas appetizer proved to be a wonderful foretaste of what would become for me a lifetime of teaching.

I need to digress for a moment to explain why I am not mentioning the names of my fellow teachers at Plainview. I don't have the chronology of my four years of teaching (with a one-year interlude in Johnstown, PA) at Plainview clearly enough in mind or on record to be sure of myself in mentioning names, dates, and events, not to mention the fact that part of the time I was dating one of the other teachers at Plainview. That was complicated. I was also part of the Beachy Amish church youth group, which added other dynamics. Life was a delicate balancing act (I was about to say "dance," but the Amish are not allowed to dance) for this single Amish boy still living at home.

To keep my own story flowing smoothly, I am writing a more general stream-of-consciousness retrospective of those years as I remember them, focusing mainly on how those experiences shaped my life and future.

What I can state with certainty is that I taught at Plainview for the four academic years of 1959-60, 1960-61, then later 1962-63, and 1963-64. The year off, 1961-62, was spent at Johnstown (PA) Mennonite School (now Johnstown Christian School), where I finally received an official high school diploma. More on that later.

Teaching at Oak Grove School was a brand-new experience. I had never attended the proverbial one-room school, nor had most of my students. It's interesting to me that the Amish community in Plain City had never built a traditional one-room school for themselves, unlike many other communities. My parents and most of the adults I knew had gone to Canaan, the local public K-12 school. Enos Stutzman says the Amish were treated fairly there and were mostly satisfied with the education at Canaan until Mr. Allison, the Principal, began showing educational films, which all the students were required to watch. That is where the Amish parents drew the line. They did not want their children watching movies! That, according to Enos, was one of the impulses leading to the building of Plainview School. Here is a photo of the now-abandoned Oak Grove School building today. (Photo by Frieda Beachy)

A one-room school is no joke. Everyone is family. There is no place to hide. You can't send any misbehaving students to the principal's office, study hall, or library. Everyone hears everything that goes on all day long. The older students help teach the younger ones. The rowdy ones disturb everyone else. We didn't even have bathrooms. There were two outhouses in opposite corners of the school yard under the oak trees. They were cold, smelly, and full of splinters. Sometimes we used old Sears catalogs and tore out pages as backup toilet paper. At recess, there were only two places for the students to go–inside or outside. By design or by default, we were thrust into a new community and became a new "family." Just like at home, if you didn't like your sister or brother, you were stuck with each other and had to work it out. The curriculum was divided into grade levels and subjects, but in effect, we were all constantly engaged in a "rolling curriculum" of ongoing learning, which all students got directly or by osmosis. There was no excuse for failing; by the time you were tested on the respiratory system in mammals, for example, you had already heard it numerous times. Don't get me wrong. Amish students are like any others. Some are curious and eager to learn, while others are just waiting for the bus to come so they can go home. But under the Amish ethos of all being equally important and none to be disrespected, we learned to help each other along, and thus instilled more than just "book-learning" in each other. There was plenty of humor and insider joking to smooth the rough edges. While the Amish held a dim view of higher education, we knew we all needed to know the basic 3 R's and the Bible to make a go of it in this life. School was mandatory until age 16, so we tried to fill grades 1-10 with useful skills and knowledge for life in our community.

On the first day of school at Oak Grove, I told the students, "This is a whole new place, and we need to learn how to do school here. You are old enough that we won't need many rules. However, the school board has made one very clear rule–nobody goes on the road without permission (the building was very close to the road). I believe that we are all mature enough that we will only make more rules if they become necessary." That sounded pretty good to everyone, and we were off to a good start. Or so it seemed. But at the first recess that morning I peeked out through the half moon hole in the door of the boys' outhouse and saw two troublemakers out on the road, running around and riding bikes, testing me on day one.

I didn't say anything, but after recess, I repeated my comments about rules and said I was very sad that two students had already decided to break the school board's rule. I asked the two, by name, to come forward and kneel at the empty front desks, facing the other students. I surprised everyone by pulling a short rubber hose from my bottom desk drawer and giving a few smart smacks to their posteriors. (This sounds harsh today, but it was a common practice among the Amish to spank unruly children with a switch, a paddle, or other object at hand. So the punishment was not unusual for the school, but my students did not expect me to be so prepared, at my young age, and on the first day back in school!) I told them to return to their seats, and the room was so quiet you could hear a mouse hiccup. We got out our math books and began learning in earnest. It was a good spring semester: a lot of learning took place, much fun was had, and deep relationships were formed that continue to this day. That is the only unhappy memory I have of the entire semester at the Oak Grove school building. My sense is that most of the students turned out fine, including the troublemakers (who became successful businessmen and are still my friends today).

I know I learned more than my students did during my four years of teaching at Plainview, and I still feel they were perhaps cheated by having this inexperienced teenager thrust upon them. But for the most part, they were very gracious, and we had a lot of good times. Story time, games at lunch, school choir, and learning to sing the "Hallelujah Chorus" for the Christmas program, vigorous and competitive softball games, and chess matches, along with rising academic levels, all stand out in my memory, and I count those four years as very special. I have always kept pictures of my Plainview days nearby and on my walls, at home and in my office. I am always glad to hear of the lifetime achievements of those students, their children, and their grandchildren. Some of their offspring intersected with my life in later years, even in Philadelphia, and I rejoice. God is good.

Perhaps the most awkward part of teaching at Plainview was that several of my siblings had to sit under the teaching of their slightly older brother. I tried to treat them just as I would any other student, but I knew human nature well enough to surmise that other students likely envied them because they got to go home every night with the teacher and get unfair homework advantages; conversely, my siblings probably felt caught in a trap–they could never get away from their teacher nor get away with anything! But my siblings are amazing and gracious; we weathered through it together and look back with mostly fond memories of those formative years. I must add that our parents taught us to be respectful and loving, setting a tone that bound us together for life and eternity–a priceless gift that explains a lot about how we got through those adventurous years. My father was a very kind man, always ready to help and hesitant to criticize. I am eternally grateful for our godly parents and their wonderful example. I still sing songs my parents sang when I was a child, and still laugh at some of the pranks we played on each other.

After becoming a teacher, I began to feel the strong need for more education. After all, the teacher should know at least a little bit more than his students. But the Amish frowned on higher education, seeing it as dangerous territory leading to the ways of the world. So the Amish had an agreement with the local authorities to run their own schools and offer only grades one through ten. After that, students obtained work permits, dropped out, helped on the farm or in a family business, and had weekly sessions with a tutor, during which they wrote summary reports of their experiential learning for that week. Learning lifetime living skills was deemed more important than getting a high school diploma. For the Plain City Amish at that time, this arrangement made sense.

But a few exceptions were allowed. If a young person wanted to become a teacher or a doctor, perhaps with careful guidance, higher education was acceptable, though it was still strewn with many potential pitfalls. So I enrolled in correspondence courses and decided to finish my high school education through correspondence while continuing to teach full-time. Needless to say, that put heavy constraints on my overloaded schedule and worked best only in the summertime. I also needed to supplement my income, so I drove the school bus and did part-time carpentry as time allowed. I had joined the Beachy Amish church by then, and as part of the youth group, I also helped with outreach and choir directing. Our church choir sang at local nursing homes and rescue missions. It was a rich and busy time.

Some years later, at a class reunion, I was sad to learn that no history of Plainview School had ever been written. I found it sad because the school has had a huge impact on the Amish Mennonite community in Plain City and beyond. That story needed to be told lest we all forget. Years later, Enos Stutzman did write that history, and we owe him a huge debt of gratitude. As the school's longest-tenured teacher and principal and an experienced writer, he was well equipped to write it. All alumni should have a copy on their shelf.

CHAPTER 6

Detour to Johnstown and Back

God had another unexpected surprise in store for me during my second year of teaching. Sanford Shetler from Johnstown, PA came to Plainview to conduct a Christian School seminar. He had done extensive research on the Christian school movement, especially among Mennonites, and encouraged many of us through his talks at the seminar. Schools other than Plainview were also in attendance. Mr. Shetler and I struck up a friendship. He was the principal and a high school teacher at Johnstown Mennonite School (JMS), now Johnstown Christian School (JCS). As we discussed our mutual passion for Christian schools and for reinforcing Anabaptist principles among the young in our Amish and Mennonite communities, he proposed a novel idea: why not have me come to Johnstown for one year to finish my high school education at JMS while also filling in a few part-time teaching slots he still had open in the elementary grades for the coming year? That sounded good to me. After prayerful consideration, my parents and the school board agreed. I knew in my soul that this was God at work. I could not have imagined such a perfect arrangement.

I moved to Johnstown, PA, in late summer 1961. It was to be another life-shaping adventure.

I moved in with the Dorsey and Joyce Thomas family, a local young Mennonite farm family who lived not far from the school. I rented a room upstairs and ate my meals with them. Joyce did my laundry, and I helped out around the place as I had time with dishes, cleaning, babysitting, etc. It proved to be a good arrangement, as they spoke Pennsylvania Dutch, attended a Mennonite church, and had a small dairy farm not that different from the ones in Plain City except that it was on a mountain, where tractors sometimes rolled out of the fields and crops had to be planted in horizontal strips around the side of the mountain to prevent soil erosion. Some local wags claimed their cows grew uneven-length legs to stand level in the fields. Living on a farm while going to school felt like home, which made the adjustment to a new environment and culture a bit easier.

Enrolling at JMS felt new and yet familiar. It was a larger version of Plainview, but with more classrooms, twelve grades instead of ten, and a mixture of Mennonite and non-Mennonite students. Also, not all the Mennonites wore plain clothing; some dressed like "the world," in my eyes. The school had an educated faculty. High school classes were held in separate rooms, including a science lab, and students had organized sports teams. While some of these new settings felt familiar, it was definitely "a step up" on the educational ladder for me.

The Mennonite community in Johnstown welcomed me into their midst. Even though I knew no one but Sanford Shetler when I arrived, I soon felt like I had a whole new family.

Joyce and Dorsey Thomas and their children made me a regular part of their family. The Carl and Lydia Kathryn Holsopple family often invited me to their house for a big family dinner after church on Sundays, as did other families. The fact that Carlene and Charlotte Holsopple were near my age and we saw each other daily in school soon made them seem like sisters to me. I got into the high school choir and some youth group activities. JMS was about twice as large as Plainview but was still made up of mostly Mennonite families who knew each other well, which made it feel like an expanding family. I forged deep friendships with classmates. I sang in men's quartets and other music groups. We took trips. I remember one trip to Pittsburgh for a

Christian concert. I remember it, not for the music, but for the cama-raderie that formed among those classmates riding with me and the fact that I almost crashed my black push-button Plymouth, as this Beachy Amish farm boy tried to navigate the narrow streets of the big city. The most ridiculous and memorable moment came when a one-eyed trol-ley headed straight toward us in the dark, and we realized I was headed the wrong way on a one-way street! The schoolmates who were with me screamed, then laughed, then never let me forget the incident after we safely backed our way out of trouble.

A major shift in perspective occurred during my year at JMS. I fell in love with the mountains! After living in the flat-as-a-pancake Darby Plains farming community in central Ohio all my life, and now adjust-ing to driving, walking, farming, navigating snow, and a host of other daily realities in the hills around Johnstown, I began to see how the mountains provided a certain picturesque quality to daily life. Driving around, looking out the window, walking to the barn—any interaction with the environment—all were subject to breathtaking panoramic shifts in scenery. The sun, moon, clouds, and changing seasons provided a constant feast for the eyes. Patterns of rain and clouds could be watched on a neighboring mountain in a way not even imaginable in Plain City. Even a helicopter view back home could not provide the striking arrays of colors seen every fall in the mountains. Life felt more poetic, almost romantic.

I had to get used to snow tires, chains, salted roads, and unsalted driveways, along with everything that comes with winter weather in the mountains. I even tried skiing with the neighbors down the hill in front of their barn. I ended up on my back when my one ski went left toward a tree, and the other came off and slid all the way down against the barn—without me! That was the last time I tried that sport. I saw how the mountains had changed me when I went back to Plain City for a visit. I realized how boring the miles and miles of flat farm land seemed after living in Johnstown for a few months. Even the Ohio Dutch sounded flatter than the folks in PA spoke their PA Dutch! My "accent" was often the butt of jokes and good-natured ridicule around JMS. I was beginning to learn how much variety there is among Mennonite and Amish communities, differences not always immediately obvious to outside observers.

As might be expected, juggling my part-time teaching, studying for my 12th-grade subjects, and having some time for extracurriculars on weekends became a juggling act. Some of my subjects were new–Problems of Democracy, for example–while others, like English and Anabaptist history, were familiar but on a more advanced level. I thrived on the adventure of new vistas beyond the Amish world I knew back home, now opening my eyes and my mind. I suddenly saw Plain City within the context of the larger national and even global Anabaptist community. I began seriously considering being a responsible citizen engaged with the problems of our democracy, learning the functions of government, and studying various ways in which the church engaged the powers.

Looking back, the year at JMS now seems like a logical extension of being thrust, as a teenager, into a teaching role back home. I can see how that year also prepared me to play a bridging role at numerous points later in my life's journey. One interesting way of framing my life story might be under the title "My Life as a Bridge." Being a bridge is sometimes necessary, useful, lonely, and painful. As my good pastor friend, Darryl Wallace, once observed, "As a bridge, you don't really belong to either shore, you stand with your feet in cold water, and people walk all over you." But a broken world needs many bridges. Arbitration, mediation, and reconciliation all require people who serve as bridges. Not to wax too theological here, Jesus was the Ultimate Bridge, and his followers should not be surprised to find themselves playing the role of mediator in a world full of broken fragments. It is truly amazing how things that make no sense at the time make a lot of sense in retrospect.

That year at JMS was wonderful and transformational. But it also precipitated a major crisis. This crisis was complicated, but let's just say that in summary, it led to a breakup with my Amish girlfriend back home, a brief dating relationship with a Mennonite schoolmate at JMS, along with a visit from my worried parents in the spring, almost making me come back home because of this turn of events. Fortunately, they were gracious and reluctantly allowed me to finish what I came for, and I graduated with a bona fide high school diploma in May 1962, at age 20. The renowned Mennonite Hour radio speaker, B. Charles Hostetter, was our commencement speaker. Several of us students also gave speeches. It was a high point in my young life.

Going back to Plain City after the school year in Johnstown brought reverse culture shock. I had discovered a new world outside the small Amish Mennonite farming community I had grown up in. Sanford Shetler had challenged all of us seniors to go forth into the world as ambassadors for Christ, to engage the world but not let its entrapments lure us off the straight and narrow path of following Jesus. To be "in the world but not of the world," as Jesus himself had taught us. The world back in Plain City was at once familiar yet foreign. I had now tasted a culture more broad-minded than my Amish boyhood, yet one that adhered to the same Anabaptist tenets of faith. This created a new dilemma for me that had begun a few years earlier. It became almost a crisis of faith. Let me explain.

You see, I had studied–and indeed taught–Anabaptist history from a series of thin booklets that Plainview used to orient us to the main outlines of our faith history. We learned about the Protestant Reformation and how the Anabaptists wanted to reform even the reformers. How they insisted on returning to the New Testament church and following Jesus alone, not the trappings and traditions of the Roman Catholic, Lutheran, and Reformed churches. It provided a general background on our Amish life and customs, helping us understand that, from the very beginning, we were "different" and did not conform to the world around us. We understood that the forefathers and foremothers of our faith gave their lives in brave martyrdom to remain true to their consciences as followers of Jesus, even if it meant defying the church's teachings. We knew that the key issue was rebaptism as believing adults when they had been baptized as infants in a state-controlled Catholic church. Also, Anabaptists refused to carry a sword or use violence against other people, especially in war. They practiced a humble, simple community of faith and emphasized the "priesthood of all believers," in which the Holy Spirit gave gifts to all in the church for ministry and evangelism.

But I had tasted those same teachings in a new community that sounded like my home community, yet with key differences. In the Johnstown Mennonite community, people wore more colorful clothing with fewer restrictions, drove a wide variety of cars (almost no horse-and-buggy people), and some women cut their hair and wore jewelry.

Yet they were from the same faith tradition as my own, and I could see that they were as sincere as, if not more so than, many in my home community. The church services were in English, with more upbeat singing, and occasionally included dramatic skits and plays. Perhaps the most exhilarating difference for me was the consistent emphasis on evangelism and missions. These Mennonites thought we were all supposed to be witnesses for Jesus among our neighbors and coworkers, invite them to church, and expect some to become followers of Jesus and join our church.

They sent missionaries overseas, heard their stories when they were home on furlough, took regular offerings for them, and even planted new churches in the city and surrounding towns! This was very exciting to me, as Esther Hilty and other Plainview teachers had taught us from the Bible that Jesus gave us the Great Commission and expected us to "go and make disciples of all the nations." This stirred a fire and a calling in my soul. I knew the Amish simply believed in "letting our light shine" quietly, and as my dad put it, if we went out to win the world, the world would ultimately win us. In fact, when he learned that I felt called to mission work, he said the Great Commission was given only to the twelve apostles and was not meant for us. (He later changed his mind and became very supportive of our work abroad and in Philidelphia.)

So now I had seen how a different Mennonite community lived out the same sense of call and even celebrated the church's spread in ways that made my church back home seem a bit sleepy by comparison. What was I to do with my new window on the world and the church? How could I go back and teach at the Amish school and just fit in as I did before? What was I to say to this whirlwind in my soul as I faced students eagerly waiting for answers to their own questions in the classrooms at Plainview? Ironically, it was the dozens of questions of my students that helped shape my faith during these mind-stretching years. ("Where in the Bible does it say we can't wear baseball caps?" "Why do we have to paint our buggies black?")

As I turned to the scriptures and to our ministers in the church for answers, I found that many of their questions could not be satisfactorily answered except by tradition. This reminded me of a similar time in the life of the young Martin Luther when he eventually nailed his 95 theses to the door in Wittenburg, Germany. He had to decide between following the traditions of the church he grew up in and following the newly awakened dictates of his own conscience. Such inner crises of faith stir both ecstasy and agony in the life of any earnest young believer, and I was no exception. The decisions I was about to make would shape the contours of my life.

My last two years at Plainview after JMS were rich and eventful. I tried to keep a long-distance relationship going with the young Mennonite woman from Johnstown while my former Amish girlfriend was on staff with me at the school. That was awkward, to say the least. But we had already established a good rapport as a close-knit staff before I left, so we simply stayed in our professional roles, and life at Plainview went on pretty much as usual. Of course, it was awkward for the students and friends back home as well. I remember being asked quite directly by some, "Do you think your former relationship, the breakup, and now the new relationship–were these all God's will for you?" I wrestled quite deeply with that one; as a spiritual leader and teacher, it was important to them and to me that this all make sense from a biblical, faith-development perspective. I think I said then (and I would still say now) that God taught me a lot during that sequence of events, and that, yes, he was leading me all along. Life's trajectories often do not follow a clean, straight line, but often trace more of a zig-zag line on one's faith map. This can be quite disconcerting, especially to young believers who think God should just lay everything out in simple, clear categories. Even Paul was redirected at times on his missionary journeys, even when he had been following clear directions from God, according to the record in Acts.

We had many great times those last two years at Plainview. We even expanded the curriculum to allow some bright students to work ahead and take 11th and 12th grade subjects on their own under my guidance (now that I had an official high school diploma myself!), learned to sing the Hallelujah Chorus from Handel's *Messiah* in the choir as well as in our youth group at Bethesda (the Beachy Amish church I was part of during my Plainview years). Many of the relationships with students and fellow young adults at church became deep and long-lasting. Most of those still hold today; even when I meet some I haven't seen in years, our hearts instantly reconnect. Some now show up as my "friends" on Facebook–a priceless gift that keeps my community of faith networked over time and distance.

I was still living at home with my parents, next door to the school, for those last two years, even though I had come of age. At age 21, Amish youth were considered adults and fully responsible for making their own decisions. Our parents and pastors, of course, hoped that we would remain in the fold and follow the path laid out for us by our faith traditions. But there was a recognition that we had more freedom to choose after age 21. Out of respect for my parents, I waited until I was 21 to make major changes. I'm glad I did, as that helped preserve our relationships going forward. I wanted my parents, friends, and students to know I was leaving, not in rebellion but in respectful obedience to my conscience. In my 21st year, I made some tough but important decisions, as we will see. Fortunately, God surrounded me with sincere praying friends who helped me discern God's will as events unfolded. In the following chapters, I will lay out several examples to clarify just how real this was for me, and to show that I was truly never alone.

I should point out, before beginning the next chapter, that my oldest siblings were dating and planning to marry, while my long-distance relationship with the young woman from Johnstown ended. I was now the older brother living upstairs at home without a girlfriend or a clear life map, while all around me things seemed to be going on as usual. Mom even became a bit nervous and quietly let me know I had better be looking for a new girlfriend before I was too old! But she and I both knew by now that my unpredictable life was likely to stay that way for a little longer. My life wasn't the only one that was changing. There was a slow and steady mass exodus from the Old Order Amish going on in that little Plain City community.

My parents and most of my near relatives, even Grandpa Hostetler, had left the Old Order Amish and joined the Beachy Amish or Conservative Mennonites. We were all riding the crest of what could be called an "Amish revival" sweeping our community, which in retrospect I am now convinced was started or at least aided by my grandfather, Joe Doddy Miller (who was still an Old Order Amish preacher but had by now moved to Iowa and remarried some years after Grandma Miller died). So my life-altering decisions were made in a state of flux, as many people around me were making big decisions, which meant leaving the Amish came at a time when many others were doing the same. I emphasize this to explain why my parents, grandparents, and peers were not as surprised by many of my decisions as they might have been in a more stable Old Order Amish community. All of us were on a journey of spiritual discovery. A deeper spiritual life was unfolding inside and around us, with no one quite sure how it would all end. Unsettling and uncertain at times, but not nearly as traumatic as being shunned by the church as a rebel, to be sure.

CHAPTER 7

Leaving the Amish to Go to College

If you add the Amish practice of shunning (or the "ban"), the idea of leaving becomes even more daunting. Any baptized Old Order Amish church member who leaves the church is excommunicated (barred from communion), and cut off from close fellowship with family and other church members. For example, one might still go home for Thanksgiving, but have to sit at a separate table. This strict form of church discipline is usually done only as a last resort and is done with the hope that the erring member will repent, confess, and be restored to the fold. The prospect of being shunned by one's family and church is a powerful deterrent, keeping many young people from even considering leaving. The pain and mental torment of living under the "ban" can produce lifelong scars.

My case was different. My parents were Old Order Amish when I was growing up, so I grew up in the Old Order Amish church. But I was never a baptized member. I was baptized at age 18 into the "Beachy Amish" church, a more progressive branch of the Amish that allowed black cars, electricity, telephones, rubber-tired tractors, and did not practice shunning. By that time, my parents and many of my relatives were also leaving the Old Order church, many joining the Beachy Amish or Conservative Mennonite churches in the community. This meant that, gradually, the shunning group became smaller than the group being shunned, which, of course, minimized its effectiveness. This massive shift was taking place when I started teaching at Plainview. That explains how I managed to have a car during my year in Johnstown.

In an interesting way, our classic 1953 Jubilee Ford tractor illustrates the transitions my parents and relatives were going through. When I was eleven years old, my father decided to get a second tractor, in addition to the Oliver Row Crop 70 we already owned. At some point, we got rid of our team of farm horses and went to all-tractor farming. Our Amish church allowed tractors for field work, as long as they had steel wheels instead of rubber tires. It's another example of Amish churches drawing the lines of separation from the world at different places, depending on the district and church you belonged to. The degrees of freedom or tolerance decided how "conservative" or "progressive" your particular Amish district was considered to be. There was no deep theology behind it for the most part. One of my uncles explained that they joined the Beachy church "because we wanted a car."

When my father decided to buy a new bright red-and-grey Jubilee Ford tractor in 1953, just like the shiny pictures I saw in *Farm Journal* magazine, I was blown away. The new design made the tractor look like a rocket about to take off, not like the typical engine-with-wheels machines we were used to. How could an Amish farmer, who insisted on painting all cars black, consider such a worldly invention? When they delivered our new tractor, my eyes were bursting with excitement. We were about to have the newest tractor in the neighborhood! My elation was soon deflated when they unloaded it, removed the wheels, and left our tractor without wheels. I felt further dejected when I saw the tractor had no headlights or taillights, as my dad thought you should work during the daytime and rest at night. Who needs lights on a tractor? Soon we had steel wheels on that Ford, which looked a lot less like a rocket then! I also remember one evening after dark when I was sitting on the front of the Ford, holding a gasoline camping lantern so my dad could finish planting beans, wondering if Dad's convictions were wavering. Eventually, we added rubber tires and lights, as shown in the photo.

Is that tractor still Amish? Am I? Is the barn (dismantled since)? The farm?

Here is a photo of me and my siblings around our trusty Jubilee Ford tractor, which my brother Lonnie still uses on the farm, taken about a decade ago.

When I had first mentioned the idea of leaving the Amish to become a missionary, my father told me to put that idea aside, as Jesus meant the Great Commission (Matthew 28–the command to "go and make disciples of all nations") only for the Twelve Apostles, not for us. When I noticed cars passing on the highway and commented on them, he told me not to think about them, as that can lead to temptation. He then proposed that he and I spend the next winter building a brand-new buggy for me, so I would have a suitable vehicle for going on dates. It was typical for the Amish to give their dating-age boys a horse and buggy and their girls bedroom furniture sets, helping them prepare for adulthood. I was torn: I felt a call from God to become a missionary, but I also wanted to respect my parents. I decided to wait to go to college until I was 21. This was the "coming-of-age" marker in our community, as mentioned above.

My dad and I spent that winter making my new buggy. It was quite a fancy buggy, "state of the art" for the time. It featured tight, sliding curtains that retracted into the cloth-lined ceiling, a built-in propane heater (with the tank behind the back seat), a varnished-wood dashboard (made by our local Amish cabinet shop), complete with a storage compartment, turn signals, and a clock. There were also outside headlights, taillights, and green rooftop lights in front (battery behind the seat). The interior was fully lined and upholstered, making for a comfy ride, day or night, any time of the year. I am not sure whether the local bishop approved of all these fancy trimmings. I was happy with my new buggy, but had mixed feelings, as it seemed that Dad was using it as a "lure" to keep me Amish. The struggle between honoring my parents and following my call to missions was intensifying. I prayed for God to guide me through this inner turmoil. What happened next seemed like a partial answer, perhaps.

That new beauty did not last long. On one of my first dates with the new buggy, I borrowed my grandfather's young horse to match my new buggy (our trusty old horse was embarrassingly slow by then). After the hymn sing or youth event of the evening, my date and I went to her home, and I tied the horse to the barn, still hitched to the buggy. It was a warm summer evening, so my date and I sat on the front porch, talking. All of a sudden, there was a terrible crash out near the barn. Frantic hoofbeats came racing out of the driveway and down the road into the summer night, scattering bits of harness, mailboxes, and wire fence as my borrowed prancing steed raced off into the darkness. The sleeping men and young boys of the house jumped out of bed, grabbing flashlights and camping lanterns as we raced out to the barn, only to find my new buggy upside down on the driveway, a pile of toothpicks! As we stood there pondering this sudden disaster, a car slowly crept into the driveway, its parking lights on, and came to a stop near where we were examining the mess. It was my cousin, Nelson Miller, and our mutual friend, Mose Gingerich, who slowly got out of the car and began to apologize.

The caption reads, "This is the picture of the wrecked buggy of Freeman Miller, which happened on the evening of July 26, 1959."

They explained that they had parked Nelson's car along the road a short distance away and tiptoed out to the barn to mess with my horse and buggy as a prank. They had planned to unhitch the reins from the bridle so I couldn't steer on my way home, a most dangerous idea! The horse was unfamiliar with them, this farm, and even with me to some extent, so he tore loose and took off for points unknown, which was fortunate for me, as I could have already been inside that buggy when it wrecked. We three guys got into Nelson's car and drove all over the neighborhood trying to locate my runaway horse, but to no avail. The next day the horse was discovered in the barn with other horses on an Amish farm about a mile from my parents' house. I wonder what stories those horses might tell about their night, if horses could talk. They must have had a few surprises of their own. In recent years, a photo of my wrecked buggy surfaced and I include it here as proof that I did not make up this wild story.

I don't know if my dad and Nelson's dad ever settled accounts, nor do I know if my grandfather's horse suffered from PTSD, nor how we got my mangled wreck home. I do know that my father never suggested rebuilding my buggy or building a new one. I like to think he may have taken it as a sign from God that I was indeed called to leave home and pursue my calling. I felt sad to see it wrecked but also felt a bit of relief, as it pointed in a direction forward.

I began teaching at Plainview that fall, so it was a busy summer of preparing for new ventures.

Joining the Beachy Amish, as the first step, had not been too difficult, since, as I said, so many of my friends and family were doing the same. After all, the Beachy Amish were still in the fold, inside the culture and language, with fewer lifestyle restrictions. But eventually I realized that I would need to leave them also, as they were not ready at that point to embrace higher education and full-scale missions. They had begun local outreach to nursing homes and rescue missions, and even sent a few persons to start new churches elsewhere. But the Beachy Amish model of church planting remained, and perhaps still remains, more of a "colonizing" one. Instead of sending one or two families into an unchurched area of the world to bring new people to faith and begin a fellowship of new believers in the cultural dress of that particular context, the Beachy Amish were more likely to send enough families and young singles into a new location where they could begin a new "colony" of Beachy Amish, hoping to eventually draw some local folks into the fold but without changing the Beachy Amish culture, dress, or worship style. In some ways that is quite understandable, since the Amish had a long history of being persecuted and driven from place to place. It was traditional to stick together in isolated, closed communities and expect to be separate from, and even misunderstood by, the world around them.

When I finally approached my Beachy Amish pastors with the heart-felt conviction that I was to go to college and prepare for the mission field, I was pleasantly surprised–and relieved–that they suggested I join a Mennonite church and not start a new trend among the Beachy Amish youth. They said they could tell from my work at Plainview School and with the church youth group that my faith was sincere. They seemed ready to bless me in pursuing my calling–just not at this church. Thankfully, I have been able to keep up mostly good relationships with the Beachy Amish churches in Plain City even until now. I was surprised many years later to be asked to preach at several of those churches back home and to be warmly received as I did so. That still amazes me. I should also note that there has been a "great awakening" among the Beachy Amish–and even among some Old Order Amish–with much more openness to new ways of expressing one's faith, along with a growing support for evangelism and missions.

Slowly, step by step, God was confirming my call to missions by opening doors along the way that I could not reasonably have foreseen: the wonderful Mennonite teachers at Plainview who first stirred the call within me, the incredible opportunity to finish high school in Johnstown, the buggy wreck, the affirmation of my Beachy Amish pastors, and the warm support of Dan Yutzy and many others at United Bethel Mennonite Church, which I soon joined. But one large obstacle remained: finances. How would I possibly pay for college, having earned a very meager salary at Plainview and having lived off my parents' generosity at home these past few years? This obstacle loomed very large, and I told God so. I said if this call was indeed from God, he would need to open this door as well. Even so, it came as a huge surprise when a dear young couple from the community came to me, saying they had heard about my sense of call and that God had nudged them to finance my way through college! I should consider it a loan to be repaid if my call to missions didn't work out. But if I ended up fulfilling that call, it would be a gift to be used in fulfilling the mission, passing the blessings along to others. I was dumbstruck! With this miraculous confirmation,

I moved forward with confidence in pursuing a college education and a career in missions. I am eternally grateful to that dear couple and still marvel to this day at how God answers prayer. Since they wished to remain anonymous, I will honor their wishes.

Below is a photo of me, as teacher, with my students at Plainview School, where I taught for four years before leaving the Beachy Amish to join the Mennonites and go off to college.

In the summer of 1964 I joined the United Bethel Conservative Mennonite Church (part of Conservative Mennonite Conference at that time) and enrolled at Ohio State University. This was a major change in my life, even though I still commuted to OSU from home. Later that fall, I did move away when I transferred for one year to Eastern Mennonite College (now University) in Harrisonburg, VA. "Leaving" the Amish then gradually became a physical reality. I was beginning to enter a brave new world, both geographically and relationally.

But first, let me describe that summer of 1964 at OSU, before I transferred to EMC in the fall. The summer of 1964 was one of gradual changes for me. I began leading congregational singing for worship at United Bethel (UB) church, which seemed normal to me because I had led singing for years at Plainview and directed the youth choir at Bethesda (Beachy Amish) Church. I didn't realize that standing up front and conducting with my hand while leading the singing was revolutionary at UB, but I later heard that I was doing something new. In those days, there was no piano nor any other instrument in church. The song leader simply started the songs, not really "directing" in the literal sense. I began to wear suit coats with buttons (still plain-cut, no lapels or ties) and got my hair cut a bit shorter and "shingled" (tapered in the back). My black car ('56 Olds, originally brown, but I had painted it black in Beachy Amish regulation) stood out in the parking lot, as UB allowed cars of various colors–even some two-toned ones! But most in the church had come from Amish backgrounds, like me, and we still spoke Pennsylvania Dutch to each other, even though the singing and preaching were in English. We knew the Amish and Mennonite families in the Plain City community. So church life was a gradual and mostly pleasant change.

Attending college classes at OSU was a more complex transition. The Ohio State University, with its 30,000-plus students, acres of campus, buildings, libraries, and classroom buildings, was an amazing new world for me. I carried a campus map most of that first summer, trying to find my way around the "city within a city." I could not believe all the academic and extracurricular options that confronted me daily. Just looking at the thousands of books in the stacks at the main library took my breath away. How could there be this much wisdom/learning/ knowledge in this little part of God's universe? Plain City, while only 25 miles away, seemed to be an ocean or two from OSU. And yet I traveled between these two worlds on a daily basis. I would bring my trusty '56 Olds to campus in the morning, find a parking lot with some free spaces, and walk several blocks to class. I remember that first quarter at OSU as being a hot summer, but most of the buildings were air-conditioned.

That is why Dan Yutzy's generosity was so deeply appreciated. Dan, our Assistant Pastor at UB in Plain City, was working on his PhD in sociology and had his own office in the Disaster Research Center, located under the stands in the football stadium at OSU, fondly called "The Horseshoe." There was a suite of offices where the DRC did voluminous research on natural disasters and human responses to them. Dan and his team would often travel to recent disaster areas and return with pages of recorded field notes, which DRC secretaries would transcribe for ongoing analyses and responses. There were a few empty offices that summer, and Dan offered that I could study in one of them between classes in air-conditioned comfort whenever I needed to. That was a great gift — to have a trusted friend and pastor from Plain City to help me adjust to college life and to offer me a cool, quiet place to study when I needed it. That stadium became a focal point that summer, as we shall see, and holds a special place in my heart to this day.

The highlight of that summer was my discovery of the angel who would eventually become my wife. This beautiful story seems like a miracle, especially since Naomi had said she would never, ever marry any-one from Plain City, especially an Amishman! So I had two huge strikes against me, but God is known for "making a way when there is no way," as my neighbors in North Philly love to say! Hallelujah!

The story goes like this: When Naomi came home from Eastern Mennonite College (now University) that summer, I already knew her as Mark Peachey's daughter and a good musician, since she and I had both been in music groups or events in the past, but I had not really looked at her in her full potential or as a possible life partner. Until that summer. One Sunday at church, she got up front to lead worship, and lo, an angel! She looked stunningly beautiful and graceful as she directed the congregation, but lofty and flowing, like heavenly breezes caught up in a cosmic symphony of beauty and soul! I could never look at her the same way after that. But it took God's prevenient grace to get us together. I wanted to ask her for a date, and told God that if she was the one for me he should please give me a good opportunity to ask her out at church the next Sunday. Our youth group and a visiting church youth group held a fellowship lunch in the basement after worship that Sunday. God gave me the most perfect chance in the world, as she and I ended up sitting near each other and talking during the meal. But I could not bring myself to ask her out. I felt sure she would turn me down. I blew the very sign that I had asked God for! Alas, woe is me, for I am undone!

I went home and fell on my knees in my bedroom, crying out to God. During my wrestling match with God, as I agonized and confessed my failure, I slowly came to my senses and realized that if it really was the will of God, there might be a second chance. That chance came sooner than I expected.

The very next morning, when I went to see Dan Yutzy at OSU and studied in that cool office between classes, he casually asked if I had heard that one of our young ladies from UB had started working there that Monday morning? No, I had not, so he took me down the hall to the secretarial pool at the Disaster Research Center. There, he introduced me to none other than Naomi Peachey, smiling at her typewriter in her new summer job! Wow, it felt like God was emphasizing a point. Lesson learned. We chatted, and she later came over to see me during her lunch break at the office, where I was studying. That is when I asked her for our first date. She said yes! We have been dating ever since. What an amazing God we serve!

That first date was a memorable event. I asked her to join me, two of my friends, and their girlfriends for a triple date to an upcoming classical music concert by the OSU orchestra at Mershon Auditorium on campus. That triple date would likely have been memorable in any case, but it turns out the other two girlfriends backed out at the last minute, and poor Naomi ended up being the only woman among the three of us young men! She has held her own quite well ever since. I still marvel at the way she holds her own in any group, with dignity and grace. We have never quite let Nelson Miller and Mose Gingerich (yes, the same two who had caused my buggy wreck!) forget how they let us down by allowing their girlfriends to back out of that wonderful first "official" date of ours (Fun fact: the three of us have remained tight friends all our lives. All three of us got married in the same year and have gotten together to celebrate milestone anniversaries several times, although we live in three separate states.).

Ironically, I ended up rooming with Nelson and Mose at EMC that fall, after transferring from OSU and moving to Harrisonburg, VA, to experience life at a Mennonite college, where Naomi, Nelson, and Mose were already enrolled. I had known Mose and Nelson all my life, as they were part of the tight group of friends I was in for most of those wonderful years at Plainview School. Nelson, Mose, John Gingerich, Ervin Troyer, and I were inseparable during those formative years, often eating lunch together and hatching any number of shenanigans.

Back at OSU that summer, one of my most vivid memories of my first taste of college was my creative writing class. I had tried my hand in short-story writing in the BookWorm Club at Plainview and loved to write, so I was quite sure this would be an exhilarating class for me. Much to my embarrassment, my first writing assignment was read aloud by the professor in front of the whole class to show how completely I had missed the exercise's intent. I had written in a completely different genre from that specified in the instructions. I can't remember the specifics, but I can easily remember my total embarrassment. But the professor, who turned out to be an atheist, took me under his wing and coached me into loving English enough to earn an "A" in the course, and eventually I decided to become an English Education major! I think he had mercy on me when he found out that I came from an Amish school and had a weak background in English. So even though he openly doubted the existence of God and said so frequently in class, he nevertheless showed respect for the common dignity of humanity and did not let our religious differences stand in the way of helping me get a good liberal arts education. I have never forgotten that valuable example when working with people of various religious or irreligious persuasions.

I had a hard time choosing a major and decided to go into pre-medicine, hoping to eventually become a missionary doctor in Africa. I later changed my major several times, first to music, and later to secondary education with an English major and German minor. I decided that teaching was my natural gift and that I could serve God as a "missionary" in many ways, as a teacher, at home, or abroad, or both. Youthful idealism gradually gave way to more adult realism, and it turns out education was a good choice, equipping me for the many aspects of teaching and preaching that would become my life.

College was certainly transformative. But not in the way I had been warned. Plain City skeptics said "those atheists" would eat me alive, leaving my faith in tatters. I found that my faith was indeed challenged in some of my classes and by the many new classmates I got to know. But I found them to be ordinary human beings, like me, trying to make sense of the life we experience together on this amazing planet. Many were intrigued by my Amish background and wanted to learn all they could from a "live" specimen. I learned that if my faith was authentic, anchored in scripture and lived experience, this new "testing" was actually one way to strengthen it.

Later that fall, during that one year at EMC, it began to dawn on me that Ohio State might actually be a "safer" place for this Amish transplant than EMC. At the Mennonite school, most people at the time came from communities or backgrounds where Anabaptist principles were at least generally known and accepted, even though there were many disagreements about their application, especially in matters of attire and "separation from the world." Professors knew people from Naomi's and my home communities, so we were expected to believe and behave in certain ways. I remember one example when I asked an "innocent" question in a New Testament class, but the professor shook his head and said, "What would Shem Peachey say?" Shem Peachey was Naomi's grandfather, a well-known leader in the Conservative Mennonite Conference. I was taken aback and decided to be more careful as to what questions I raised. At OSU, on the other hand, it was clear that "higher education" included the freedom to ask any question you wished, as long as you provided thoughtful approaches to finding good answers. Whenever fellow students or professors at OSU found out about my Amish background, they would be genuinely intrigued and want to ask all kinds of sincere questions, while I was expecting to be ridiculed for being "backward" and ill-informed.

After that year at EMC, Naomi and I both decided to transfer to Ohio State University. We were both interested in the city, and we both had family living near Columbus. Since OSU used the quarter system, I could continue pursuing my bachelor's degree year-round, including summers. OSU was also much less expensive and offered good work-study options to supplement our income. It seemed like a good fit. So we moved back home to Ohio that summer of 1965, and I continued taking courses, as Naomi again worked at the Disaster Research Center.

That fall of 1965 at OSU, I moved into the "Menno House," a house near campus owned and operated by Neil Avenue Mennonite Church (now Columbus Mennonite), intended primarily as an off-campus residence for Mennonite male students, while Naomi moved into an off-campus apartment with female roommates. I moved in with Wayne Yutzy from Plain City as my roommate, which helped me feel less "alone" since Wayne and I shared roots and heritage. We were from two different but similar conservative Mennonite churches in Plain City, so we represented that culture in an international, intercultural house of undergrad and grad students. Other Mennonites were there from various communities in Ohio and the eastern US, but some were from other parts of the world.

One who became a very good friend of mine was from Dhamtari, India, and from a large, well-established Mennonite community there. He was the principal of the Mennonite high school in Dhamtari and came to the US for his master's degree. Jehoash Harishandra was a devout Christian, and I loved comparing notes with him, as we had both been teachers and principals at Mennonite schools. He helped me see the world through the eyes of a fellow Anabaptist from an Asian perspective. Another international student who also became a good friend was Ganga Prasad Dass from Nepal. He was not a Christian but a Hindu, as I recall, which led to many discussions comparing various religions that did not seem to impress him. But when he went with us to see a film on the life of Jesus, he was mesmerized. I realized then that a simple encounter with Jesus can often be more powerful than theological persuasion.

Even though we were both Secondary English Education majors, Naomi and I had very few classes together. Since my minor was German, I took German classes, and she took psychology classes for her minor. Most of our common experiences were extracurricular. For example, we both became OSU football fans for life, even though we knew very little about football before then. Go, Buckeyes!

The courses we took at OSU were generally very good. We learned a lot about how to learn, how to teach, and how to appreciate good writing, music, and art. A well-rounded liberal arts undergraduate degree in education, with a focus on language and literature, was great preparation for a life of service and ministry at home or abroad. It also provided a good foundation for my later graduate work at Eastern Mennonite Seminary and in urban studies at Temple University. OSU was a great place to rethink my beliefs about best practices for living out Anabaptist principles in our modern world. OSU was ideal for this because we lived in several worlds at once. We went home to Plain City for many family and church events, but we also attended Burnside Mennonite Church on the edge of Columbus, in a Black community. We also met people from everywhere at a major urban university. This combination provided many opportunities to test various expressions of faith and to see which of our home practices made sense away from home and which needed to be modified. Wearing distinctive clothing as a symbol of nonconformity to the world was strongly emphasized in our community back home. That became an issue for us in our new urban context. The photo below of our wedding shows how we dressed for formal occasions in 1966, between our junior and senior years at OSU. (The Amishman in front of the bald man is my paternal grandfather, "Joe Doddy" Miller, next to his second wife.)

A few examples will illustrate what I mean about dress issues. My plain coat and Naomi's prayer veiling were obvious markers of faith that made sense most of the time back home but often caused confusion elsewhere. My encounter several years earlier with a Navy officer at the Miami airport on my way to visiting my Beachy Amish missionary friends in Hattieville, Belize, was perhaps the most jolting. The officer began reprimanding me for wearing only part of my Navy uniform, which was strictly forbidden. He thought my button-down Beachy Amish pants were a part of a Navy uniform. One wore the entire uniform, or none of it! He thought I was in the Navy, and his surprise was hilarious when he learned that I was Amish. He apologized profusely, began explaining how wonderful the Amish were, and revealed many typical misconceptions about them. For me, it illustrated just how our symbols can have opposite meanings depending on the context: at home, my plain clothes symbolized my separation from the world and, certainly, from the military, but here in a metropolitan airport, it apparently did the exact opposite. This meant that some soul-searching and rethinking were in order.

Other examples happened on campus at OSU. Naomi and I sang in the huge college chorale, and one year we helped perform Handel's "Messiah," with some Plain City friends in the audience. I wore my plain suit, and she wore a dress along with her usual prayer veil, which we did whenever we dressed up for church or formal occasions. At such times, it was not unusual for people to ask her if she was a nurse or a nun; they would ask me if I was a monk or a priest. Also, we would walk around on campus holding hands, or drive around in our car together. After our marriage, we would go to and from our near-campus apartment together. Clearly, our symbols were not always conveying the intended meaning, and we began to realize how strange we must appear to people on campus or around town — a priest and a nun holding hands and apparently living together in an apartment!

So, gradually we began to change: I wore a lapel coat with no tie (at first) and later with a tie. Naomi mostly wore her prayer veil at church, not for everyday activities. Coming from our Amish and conservative Mennonite backgrounds, we found these changes very difficult, as the teachings we grew up with placed a strong emphasis on nonconformity to the world around us — and on wearing the symbols of that nonconformity without shame or apology. Our inner struggles as we made these changes were not easy to shake. How could we live our convictions in ways that made sense in our new settings? Contextualizing our beliefs and practices became an ongoing process as we moved from place to place over the years. Overseas missionaries–and any cross-cultural workers, really–constantly wrestle with these issues also.

By far the best thing that happened to us at Ohio State was our marriage. God knitted our lives together in ways that I could not have imagined. From our first date to the night of our engagement, we sensed God leading us, providing support through wonderful people, turning many improbabilities into realities, eventually culminating in our unforgettable wedding day. In our last year of college, Naomi and I were able to experience marriage and college life at the same time. It was a great year!

Our wedding was a memorable moment that brought our various worlds together. The wedding itself was held at United Bethel church near Plain City, with Assistant Pastor Dan Yutzy (whose office at OSU had led to our first date) preaching the wedding sermon. Naomi's father, Bishop Mark Peachey, performed the vows. Many of my family and friends, including my parents, grandfathers, uncles, aunts, and cousins, as well as former Plainview students, sat on one side, while Naomi's family and friends, including most of United Bethel church, sat on the other. The church youth group provided special acappella music from the balcony, directed by Nathan Showalter. Our bridal party included family members and friends from both sides. To me, the day was a miracle because it brought together such an incredible mix of people and networks from both of our pasts. There were no musical instruments except a pitch pipe, as none were allowed at UB at that time. No ring ceremony, either, as rings were considered worldly jewelry and likewise forbidden.

The reception was held at Rosedale Bible Institute (now College), near Naomi's parents' home. After the ceremony, everyone needed to drive twelve miles to the reception, where there was sufficient room in the dining hall to serve all the guests. I well remember the awesome feeling of having all our worlds come walking through the doors of our receiving line, including my two surviving grandfathers — Joe Doddy Miller and Mose Doddy Hostetler — along with our extended families, friends, and associates from all over. As they were shaking hands with our bridal party, I wondered what they thought about the unusual mix of people from Plain City, Columbus, Rosedale, and beyond. The importance of celebrating this important milestone with all of those in our faith community was unmistakable, a once-in-a-lifetime moment to cherish forever. In those days, it was still customary to open the gifts after the meal, naming the gifts and givers for all to enjoy, which added to the celebratory spirit of the day.

Getting away from the reception and out of town was another matter. We had arranged to have our car carefully "hidden" in my parents' garage, but the Gingerich brothers managed to "find" it. They added the usual decorations, including a string of empty tin cans tied to the rear bumper, which would rattle and clatter as we drove away. Eventually, we drove off into the sunset and headed south (without GPS, of course), planning our honeymoon as we went.

We knew we wanted to go somewhere in the South, but where? With a few maps in hand, we simply started driving, choosing our destination when we felt we had reached it. We had the Great Smoky Mountains in mind as a romantic section of the country where we could find a cabin in the woods for a week. On our meager budget, we would need to find something simple and inexpensive. That was fine with us, as we had God and each other. That was enough. We could celebrate anywhere, as long as we were alone and together. Our little blue American Rambler headed down the highway, and we were full of joy, ready to explore the wonderful world of married life.

One of the questions we had wrestled with was whether or not to wear wedding rings after we were married. Since rings were not allowed at United Bethel, we could not hold a ring ceremony, so we came up with a compromise. In our new urban world, wedding rings were very important symbols of a high view of marriage, a sign that you took your vows seriously and wore a daily, public expression of that commitment. We believed all of that deeply and were eager to wear that expression publicly. But we wanted to be sensitive to the cultures and worlds our families were part of as well, not flaunting our new freedom in front of them too quickly.

Here is how we handled our dilemma: we kept our rings in the car's glove box, only putting them on when we arrived at the hotel for our first night as a married couple. Again, this was no easy decision, as we were pushing the edges of our church "rules," but we wanted the hotel manager to know we were a married couple as we rented a room. We also assumed we would soon join a church where rings were not an issue. This was one more transitional compromise as we navigated our journey between worlds.

We finally ended up somewhere in the Smoky Mountains and spent a day or so, but decided it wasn't quite what we envisioned. So we headed our little Rambler northward, eventually ending up in a cabin beside Lake Erie in Ohio. This was more familiar territory, as my father had often taken us fishing on Lake Erie. That little cabin by the lake at Mari-Dor Beach in Vermilion, Ohio, turned out to suit us just fine, a welcome break before we returned to Ohio State to finish our last year of college.

Back on campus, we spent our last undergraduate year in our small apartment on the edge of campus, across from Arps Hall. I won't go into great detail about that year, which I spent juggling marriage, church, classes, graduation, and preparation for three years in Nigeria after graduation. Occasionally, we entertained visitors from Plain City, especially young people who were beginning to explore college life. We enjoyed late-night Rook games when Naomi's brother, Titus, came to spend the night, listened daily to Paul Harvey News on the radio, and began planning for our futures as teachers overseas.

Both of our student teaching experiences in that final year were great learning experiences. My daily car rides with five other OSU students to the upscale high school for wealthy white kids in Upper Arlington were quite an experience. This was the same area where I had built houses with Ora Gingerich's crew, as you may recall. As OSU students, we discussed everything from atheism to education to various cultures to world events. I had a wonderful, seasoned English teacher to work with at Upper Arlington High, so the student teaching itself was quite satisfying, even though I could not imagine myself ever living and teaching in a wealthy white suburb. It was all part of my "re-formation" from an Amish farm boy to a global citizen, eager to see where God would take us next. It was almost time to graduate to the next chapter of our lives together.

Just before graduation, my father took us fishing on Lake Erie, a trip Naomi will never forget. While my father was pulling in bluegills and sunfish two and three at a time, poor Naomi could not catch a thing. They even traded fishing poles for a while, but that made no difference. Finally, Naomi just put up her pole and decided to take a nap instead. The bright sun on the water gave Naomi a sunburn, so that at graduation her face was as red as a beet as she painfully endured our important day. Commencement exercises at a large state university are massive events, and we felt rather small in that sea of seniors about to walk across the stage. We were just two among thousands. What mattered most were those red padded folders containing our bachelor's degrees. We were officially college graduates and certified to teach high school English! A milestone indeed.

As we considered various options for the upcoming year, two possibilities rose to the top: (1) I could teach English and German at a public high school in Cincinnati, Ohio, where Naomi's sister Nona and family lived; or (2) We could both sign up to teach English overseas somewhere with Mennonite Central Committee's Teachers Abroad Program. The second option won out, and MCC decided to send us to Nigeria to teach at an Anglican high school for three years. This assignment would also qualify for my alternative service to the military, as a conscientious objector to war. It seemed like a good way to test whether God was calling us to long-term service in Africa. We spent the summer getting the necessary vaccinations, packing all our belongings, storing them at Naomi's parents' house, and packing two barrels of clothing and supplies that MCC would send by sea for our three years in Nigeria. We were about to venture abroad.

CHAPTER 8

Service Venture in Nigeria

This next chapter finds us suddenly airlifted out of our now-familiar urban college life, out of all our comfort zones, into a brand-new, life-changing experience on the other side of the world. We decided to sign up for a three-year assignment with Mennonite Central Committee's Teachers Abroad Program. As a conscientious objector, I needed to complete two years of service as an alternative to military service, and this assignment with MCC would qualify. MCC decided to send us to teach English at Crowther Memorial College, a secondary Anglican school in Lokoja, Nigeria, West Africa located at the confluence of the Niger and Benue rivers. Our assignment would last for three years, from 1967 to 1970.

We felt called to overseas mission work, and three years in West Africa seemed a good way to test that calling. After graduation, we began packing. We moved in with Naomi's parents in Rosedale for the summer, stored a lot of our books, clothing, and other meager belongings upstairs in their "attic" under the eaves, plus some in their tool shed. We were advised to fill one or two 50-gallon steel drums with clothing and incidentals to send to Nigeria by ship (which would not arrive for weeks), and to take a few suitcases with enough to live on until the drums arrived. It was a stressful few months of transition and preparation.

Getting ready to go overseas is a complex operation. Not only do you need the proper passports, visas, and vaccinations, but you also need to study the climate and culture of the place you are going to. What kinds of clothing are appropriate? What foods will you be able to buy? What foods will you be able to tolerate? What language barriers should you prepare for? Will you be coming back home at regular intervals, or will this be an uninterrupted time period with no regular visits or supply shipments from home? (Remember, in the late 60's there was no internet and we had no cell phones or landlines.) Can you think of starting a family, or will you need to put that on hold for three years? Should you subscribe to several of your indispensable magazines, even if they may arrive months late? Where will you live? What housing conditions may you need to adjust to? What about health concerns? Are there good doctors and hospitals available? Is your agency able to provide health coverage, or do you need to prepare in advance to cover all your own costs? What allergies or food reactions might you face? Is there a supportive church community to join? The list goes on.

When we were finally all packed up and ready to travel, we went to the MCC headquarters in Akron, PA, where we had a two-week orientation before flying to Africa. We stayed at the guesthouse, ate in the dining hall, and enjoyed excellent teaching from MCC staff and returning workers from abroad. They emphasized serving in the spirit of Christ, blending in with the local churches and agencies where we would be working, and learning the customs, cultures, and languages of our new context to be effective. We appreciated MCC's emphasis on being one with the people, learning alongside Nigerians as co-workers, and not going in with pre-packaged answers, an attitude often displayed by Westerners working in the developing world.

Naomi's parents took us to the Amtrak station in Lancaster, bound for New York, where we would catch our flight to Nigeria. A funny last moment glitch almost got Mark Peachey to go with us. He helped us carry our luggage onto the train. Before we got seated, the train started moving, and he just jumped out of the train onto the platform at the last second as the doors rolled shut, with our umbrella still in his hand! Close call. Umbrellas can be bought anywhere.

So we were finally off. I don't remember much about the train ride or the taxi ride to JFK airport, with our large stuffed suitcases and carry-ons, but I do remember what a relief it was when we were finally in the air. We were two young and healthy souls, venturing out into the great big world all alone. Having spent most of our lives surrounded by family and loving communities, we suddenly felt all on our own. We knew that MCC had people on the ground in Nigeria who would welcome us, take us to our city and school, orient us, and make sure we were safely settled. But even that felt brand new. We had never met the country director couple or the two other American Teachers Abroad Program (TAP) teachers at the school we were headed to. Also, one of the two, Bill Rappold, had sent a telegram while we were at orientation, advising us that the civil war, which had broken out, was making things very uncertain, adding, "Don't expect the Millers." Our town, Lokoja, had just been bombed, so the TAP teachers had gone to another town to await further instructions. MCC said the country director was still expecting us, so Bill may have been overreacting a bit. Naturally, our insides were churning as we headed into a war zone where it might not be safe to teach school. It was possible that MCC would reassign us to another country altogether! Our overseas sojourn had begun.

After a layover in London, our British Airways plane took off for Nigeria, with quick stops in several West African countries before finally landing in Lagos, which at the time was Nigeria's capital. I distinctly remember that first wave of warm, humid air hitting us in the face as we deplaned. The smells and sounds were different; people spoke other languages; the soil was sandy; most of the cars looked different; and they drove on the "wrong" side of the road. We were finally in the great continent of Africa! I think the Sudan Interior Mission (SIM) Guesthouse had sent a car or a cab to meet us, and the driver wound through the crowded streets of Lagos to an enclosed compound where the guesthouse was located. I vividly remember that first night. After eating a tasty supper with several missionaries, we fell into bed, totally exhausted yet energized. Sleep was slow in coming. Just as we would be drifting off, street noises, horns, sirens, and strange night sounds would startle us awake. I remember wondering what night creatures — insects, animals, birds — made those sounds I had never heard before. No one else seemed one bit concerned, so we decided all must be well and finally went to sleep in a strange bed with strange pillows, tucked inside a mosquito net suspended from the ceiling. The windows were open to let in a breeze, but it was still warm enough that we needed a ceiling fan to sleep. We had no idea what little creatures might scamper across the floor and along the walls while we tried to sleep in the African night. But we were here. We felt safe.

The next morning, our SIM hosts took us back to the airport, and we boarded a smaller Airbus plane to fly north to Kaduna, where Ivan and Mary Eikenberry — Church of the Brethren missionaries — lived. Since the Mennonite missionaries and TAP directors had all evacuated when the war broke out, the Eikenberrys were serving as country directors for MCC. We would spend a few days with Ivan and Mary before flying on to Lokoja. That was a very fortunate stopover during our first week in the country, as they were seasoned veterans who could ease our tensions, orient us to Nigerian customs, and give us a realistic assessment of the war. Their house was built of colorful cinder blocks, with concrete floors and a tin roof, like most of the houses around them, and it exuded a sense of peace where one could relax and unwind. The palm trees, flowering shrubs, and small yard all made the place very welcoming. After spending time with them, we felt ready to continue on to our assignment with calmer nerves and steadier heartbeats, ready to meet our new Nigerian coworkers.

Our next (and last) flight was on a small plane, with two missionary pilots in the two front seats. Naomi and I squeezed into the two seats in the back. The small propeller plane was not nearly as quiet nor as smooth as the jetliners, of course, and we were in for a few thrills.

Because of the war, the pilots were not entirely sure where it was safe to land, but they were going to try for a small landing strip near a town in the center of the country. To be sure it was safe to land, they circled the strip a few times, then began descending. We thought we were cleared for landing, but suddenly they pulled the plane into a sharp ascent, and I thought my stomach dropped to the floor! It was a gut-wrenching surprise, just another maneuver to be sure it was safe to land before actually doing so. (Naomi thinks they did it to scare us; they succeeded!)

Once on the ground, we had a driver waiting to take us the rest of the way to Lokoja in a jeep. We drove over bumpy dirt roads with occasional stretches of asphalt; even those stretches were still jagged and full of potholes. On these roads through the Nigerian bush, we could observe villages, tin- or thatch-roofed houses, small roadside shops, families at work, and domestic and wild animals (nothing big), all at eye level.

Strangely, I don't remember my first impressions of Lokoja. My feeling is that we may have gone to the International Guest House for a few nights before the school had the staff house ready for us. I do, however, have a very distinct early memory from one of the first evenings we were there. We were invited to Principal J. O. Ojo's house — along with other new and returning faculty members — for dinner and a time to get acquainted, orientation, etc. As I recall, we were invited to come at 6:00 p.m., which we did, and, to our embarrassment, we were the only ones there! In fact, Mr. Ojo and his wife were clearly not ready for us, needing to get dressed, finish cooking, and attend to other sundry details that gave us newcomers away. No Nigerian would presume to arrive exactly at the stated time; in their culture, "everybody knew" that 6:00 p.m. meant "sixish," anytime in the next hour, or whenever you managed to get there. We certainly learned that lesson well; I don't think we arrived early at any event ever again during our three years in Nigeria. Some experiences are quickly internalized!

Lokoja is a small West African city (population around 200,000), located at the confluence of the huge Niger and Benue rivers, near the center of the most heavily populated country in Africa, nestled between the rivers and Mount Patti, a small mountain on the edge of town. Lokoja is an unusual African city, as it "belonged" to no language group or tribe. When the British arrived, they chose Lokoja as their inland hub, hoping to spread their civilization throughout West Africa. They managed to settle freed slaves from various tribes there, building churches, businesses, and government agencies, and connecting several states via rough roads and a ferry crossing across the river. But they had not counted on nor known about the devastating power of the pesky mosquito, so many of the early pioneers and settlers died of malaria. Charles Dickens regularly made fun of the British missionaries of the day, and in his fiction, he dubbed the city of Lokoja, "Borrioboola-Gha," an obvious reference to what local Nigerian tribal languages sounded like to the British. We found a book about the history of Lokoja titled Dickens's made-up name. (London: Oxford University Press, 1960) Perhaps it is still in print, or you might find it in a dusty rare book section of a library archive.

The first months in Lokoja were mind-stretching experiences. The school, Crowther Memorial College (really a high-school-level Anglican school) supplied housing for its teachers, so there was a nice little two-bedroom cinder block and tin roof bungalow for us, just across a little creek from the school, about a quarter-mile path through the tall grass and past one or two other houses.

Our one-story house had cement floors--smooth and painted--making them cool to one's bare feet on those steamy, hot tropical days we had almost every day in Lokoja. The school was also built of cinder blocks, with cement floors, and a tin roof. It was a two-story, long, narrow building, only one classroom wide, with a veranda and walkway running alongside the full length of each floor on one side. Wisely, the building was situated so that the sun rose at one end and traveled straight across the roof ridge to the other, preventing direct sunlight from entering the windows on either side. The windows were all made of louvered glass, so they could be kept open most of the time, allowing a breeze to flow through each classroom or office straight across the building. With the tin roof reflecting much of the direct sunlight, the cooling effect of the cement floor, and the cooling breeze blowing from one side to the other, the building was about as cool as it could be without air conditioning. Even so, most of us were perspiring from early morning till late at night on most days.

Crowther Memorial College classroom building, with students lined up for morning prayers.

Even as trained English teachers, we had to learn a new vocabulary, beginning with British spellings and pronunciations. For example, laboratory now, while spelled the same, was pronounced lab-or-ATE-ory or lah-BOR-atry. I'm not sure which was British and which was the local dialect; both had to be mastered in order for us to teach our students "correct" English usage! These bright young Nigerian students were not easily convinced; they wanted to know who "owned" the English language, the Americans or the British? After all, most of their 120+ languages were the cultural property of the local village and the tribe there. These were things they did not teach us at Ohio State, even though we had degrees that made us certified teachers of English at the secondary level.

We soon learned that we were "expatriates," the term for those from other countries. Several sections of the city, as well as clubs and the international guest house, were largely designed for expatriates. Fortunately for us, the house which the school provided for us was along a main road leading into town, in a row of other houses and shops, so we had Nigerian neighbors all around us. The one exception was the compound across the road from us, which had been converted into a military barracks during the war.

We soon got used to living in constant tropical heat, with our lifestyle schedules adjusted accordingly. (Pronounced SHED-yules in British English). By the time the sun was overhead, we were in the shade and breeze of the smartly-designed building. Even so, we got used to wearing damp clothing that clung to our skin, having sweaty hair, being coated with a thin layer of brown sandy dust, cleaning our glasses often, and still running out of energy several times a day in our natural sauna. No wonder we all went home at 1:30 for lunch and siestas. No wonder all the shops and businesses closed during the hottest part of the day as well.

We needed to make many cultural adjustments, of course. I will mention a few to illustrate. At first, we closed our doors during our afternoon nap, but soon learned that students and others might drop in to visit while we were asleep, only to feel offended by our closed doors. The convention in town required an open door of hospitality; otherwise, it signaled an unwelcoming attitude. The prevailing local custom was to leave doors standing open, with a loose curtain hanging in the opening to keep out sun and insects. It was not uncommon to wake up after a siesta to find guests, including students, waiting in our living room. They often came without any stated agendas other than sharing time together. Of course, they had long figured out that time is one of the things we Westerners value most, so why wouldn't we want to share it?

Another practice among students was to show respect for teachers by offering to carry the many items teachers might bring from class to class. So the students would come running as we walked from one class to another or sometimes even as we were walking home, insisting that they should carry our books or briefcases or papers or–oh, no, Naomi's purse! That was the one thing she just could not give up. As an American woman, she carried her purse with her wherever she went. She explained to the students that her purse was for her personal items. Also, I was not expected to do any strenuous physical labor. Once, while building a cage for our two pet monkeys, I was surprised to hear several passing students remark that they had never seen an American working this hard before! Oh, my. Sad perspective. Another colonial hangover?

Corporal punishment of students was occasionally part of morning assemblies. "Caning" was often the preferred method, whippings applied with switches made from tree branches.

Mr. Ojo, the Principal, could often apply severe strokes to emphasize the seriousness of the punishment. Sometimes the offending student would scream and cry while being caned, only to make light of it later in the classroom. Sometimes, disciplinary methods jolted expatriates' sensibilities but were taken in stride by both students and teachers.

Another custom that was unusual for us was students respectfully standing whenever the teacher or principal walked into the room. After the teacher said, "Good morning, class!" the students would reply, "Good Morning, Sir! (pronounced SUH)" or "Good morning, Madam!" (pronounced mahDAHM) then take their seats, open their books, and prepare to take notes during the class. These high school students were very bright, taking notes faster than college students at OSU. They could play back, almost verbatim, anything they were taught, even music. I taught them several new songs when I directed the choir, songs like "Joy to the World" (a Christmas carol they had never heard before), only to be amazed that as fast as I sang line by line of the new song they jotted down the do-re-mi's and sang them back to me! What a thrill to conduct such a choir!

I might add that "Joy to the World" became an instant favorite, which needed to be sung each year at the Christmas program (and sometimes in between), as did "See, Amid the Winter's Snow," which was extremely hard to sing in 100-degree weather, in a tropical climate that never saw snow. But Mr. Ojo, who had earned his master's degree in London, insisted because "It was tradition!" Lokoja was a confluence, not only of rivers, but also of cultures, nationalities, and educational methods. Lecture and rote learning sometimes compete with newer styles of interactive teaching techniques. But all methods had to fit within the firmly established British educational system, which included passing a final exam at the end of each academic year to advance to the next level. Our diverse faculty of Nigerian, British, Indian, and American teachers made for a stimulating educational environment. Perhaps we learned more than our students did. All in all, we had many wonderful experiences at Crowther Memorial College. We were glad we had a three-year assignment, as the first year was mostly about learning and adjusting. By year three, we felt we were making a solid contribution and were "at home" in our context. We felt we learned so much more than any short-term missions trip could ever provide, useful though such trips might be.

Nigeria is Africa's most populous country. It has great natural resources, including huge oil fields. Its greatest resource is its people, 230 million of them in 36 states, according to 2024 statistics. We were sent there to teach high school English, the official national language. We also wanted to learn a local tribal language, but since there were seven such languages in our British-created city, we learned only a few greetings in a few of them. We spoke a lot of Pidgin English, which is what the local people used to communicate across cultures. When we were there, we were told there are over 120 languages in the country, with dozens of lesser dialects.

A typical day at Crowther began at 6:30 a.m., before the sun was high in the tropical sky, with students going to the school to cut their strip of grass with machetes on the huge school front lawn. We teachers did not have to report until around 7:30, as I recall, when classes began. There were daily Morning Prayers (chapel) when the students lined up in rows by class on the sandy driveway in front of the school, while Mr. Jiya played the pump organ to lead singing from the front veranda. There were scripture readings and prayers, as well as "inspections" of all students, row by row, to ensure their hair was neatly parted, uniforms were clean and neat, and attitudes were properly adjusted for the day. We moved from classroom to classroom in each succeeding period, as teachers, and broke only for breakfast. This continued until 1:30 when school closed for lunch and afternoon siestas. We all went to our homes, to return at 4:00 p.m. for "preps"--homework and extracurriculars, especially sports. By evening, we were all exhausted, ready for the evening meal and some much-needed sleep, if we could get comfortable in the relentless humid heat. By morning, it would start all over again.

Since we were volunteers, our earnings as teachers went straight to MCC to cover administrative costs. MCC gave us (and all TAP teachers) an allowance to live on. We learned tight budgeting by necessity, dividing our allowance cash into four or five tin cans each month (depending on how many weeks there were) and locking them in our concrete walk-in closet to stretch our allowance to the end of the month.

That was a good lesson to learn, although a bit stressful at times. I have often said — truthfully — that we went to Nigeria penniless and came back penniless, but were incredibly "enriched" by the experience. Three years seemed like a very long commitment at first, but they went by rather quickly in the whirlwind of activities.

There were four to six of us expatriates on a staff of twelve or so. All the others were Nigerians, including the principal. All the students were local Nigerians. All had to compete to get into the school and to keep their spot once admitted. That has a way of changing the educational landscape. They had to pay school fees; their parents were highly motivated to have them behave and succeed in the special privilege of getting a secondary education, not at all a common expectation in the US. It also raised the stakes for us as a private, church-sponsored school to maintain our standards and achievement levels. Any discipline was likely to work well, as anyone suspended or expelled knew that others were standing in line for their seats. Motivation was high. Kids will be kids, of course, so there were the typical slackers and pranksters one finds in any school, but the discipline tended to be much easier because the stakes were so high. Serving as a minority in such a setting is a great learning experience in itself. Any perceptions we Americans brought to current events were naturally "corrected" by our Nigerian friends, both staff and students. They were always kind and respectful, but they let us know when our "foreign eyes" were seeing events through a blur.

One such example came one day in the staff lounge as I was reading the international edition of *Time* magazine. An article and photo of the war in Nigeria showed how some in the war zone were forced to buy and eat "rats" in the local market. Our Nigerian staff members chuckled as we showed them the photo, remarking that the photo was of a fat "field rat" (perhaps similar to American muskrats), a delicacy not affordable to most Nigerians. I guess the foreign war journalist must have been thinking of sewer rats back home, not bothering to check with the market vendors before posting the photo.

Teaching English as a second language is also an education in itself. One quickly discovers that some rules of grammar make very little sense; that English is a complex language greatly influenced by words and phrases borrowed from other language families. It should be simple to explain why "bough" and "bow" can be pronounced the same but spelled so differently. Why are some letters silent? Why can vowels be long and short? Why does the subject usually come first and the verb second? The hardest things to teach turned out to be idioms and jokes. Idioms "just are" even though our students wanted logical explanations. How can you "tip your hat" to someone when you aren't even wearing one? How can you "lose your mind" when you are perfectly healthy and sane? Jokes were hilarious in all directions. Things we Americans thought hilarious might not tickle the Nigerian funny bone at all. Conversely, things that produced side-splitting laughter in the classroom might leave us completely straight-faced. Such is the fine art of communication across cultures.

Food is a great uniter or divider of cultures. Nigerian cuisine took some time to get used to. Nigerian cuisine, although very delicious, is also quite spicy hot and took some time for us to fully adjust to. We were determined to get comfortable with the local culture, so once a week, Naomi and I would go to the market and eat at a local restaurant, where the food was cooked over three stones out back. They served some of the finest rice you will ever eat, with a variety of savory sauces to choose from as toppings. Or you could choose pounded yams: large tubers peeled, cooked, then "pounded" by two women in a large wooden mortar and pestle until they formed something akin to mashed potatoes but much gummier and firmer. It came in a ball on your plate, then you broke off a lump, dipped it into a bowl with sauce, and let it slide down your gullet in one smooth, non-chewing motion. They put very hot peppers into most of their sauces, creating rivers of tears at first until we got used to them. Only bread or bananas could counter the burning sensation. Water made it worse. Eventually, we got to craving our weekly dinner out; it was one of those things we missed most when we got back home. Even today, we will rush to any Nigerian meal, hoping to find fufu, egusi soup, akara, fried plantain, and plenty of rice! American cuisine seems bland, almost tasteless, by comparison.

Nigerian culture is definitely an event-centered, rather than time-centered, culture. Every holiday, birth, visit by a dignitary, retirement, death, or move called for a huge celebration. When Mr. Ojo, our first principal, left for another assignment, the school planned a two-week going-away celebration. Every evening for two solid weeks, the school held a celebration. According to a letter I recently reread, we were responsible for coordinating all of that. (Neither Naomi nor I have a clear memory of this.) Whenever the state governor came to visit, all school activities were abruptly halted; all students and staff had to clean the entire school, compound, and everything else. We would line up along the road, waiting for him to pass, or, better yet, have him speak at the school. I remember one time in the middle of an important exam, Mr. Ojo came into the classroom and declared, "Everyone outside; the Governor is coming!" I protested that we were in the middle of an exam and needed to finish (stupid American!). He didn't bat an eye and announced that they could finish the exam tomorrow. Okay then.

A huge surprise came when I was asked to serve as Interim Principal for a month or two before the new principal, Mr. Olaoba, arrived. I certainly felt unprepared and underqualified for that role, but reluctantly complied under pressure. They wanted someone who would guide the ship with a steady hand, not making any waves, until the new administration could take over. It went well, but I was very relieved when the new principal arrived. This would turn out to be only one of several times in my life when I was called to stand as a bridge during a transition or conflict.

Another came as the war was beginning to end, and we served for a month between school terms in the war zone at Bori Hospital near Port Harcourt, as many of their staff had fled during the war. I agreed to be the interim administrator of the hospital, while Naomi filled prescriptions in the dispensary as head nurses from the various wards brought their lists of requested medications. I rather enjoyed running the hospital ambulance to and from town with lights and sirens flashing as I breezed through the many military checkpoints along the way! We heard guns and bombing in the distance, which kept us awake some nights, but one can get used to just about anything, as my Grandpa Hostetler used to say.

Although Nigeria had won independence from Britain in 1960, it was under military rule while we were there. The head of state was Lt. Colonel Yakubu Gowon, who had come to power in one of several earlier coups. In 1967, the Eastern Region declared independence as the Republic of Biafra under the leadership of Lt. Col. Emeka Ojukwu. The civil war lasted 30 months and took a huge toll. Eventually, Biafra fell, and the country was reunited. We actually had teachers from the Eastern Region who were Igbos come and join the staff at Crowther before we left in 1970. During the many long months of the war, we were used to many disruptions in daily life. Whenever even a faint airplane sound was heard (our students had heard them before we did!), all the students would scoot their wooden chairs back from their wooden desks and rush en masse outside to hide under the trees. Earlier, homemade bombs had been dropped out of small planes on Lokoja and kept the whole town skittish for months. The many military checkpoints were a great nuisance as well. Trips on rough roads and through the hot countryside were already tedious; now they were prolonged by soldiers who made us open our suitcases, all our documents, and answer all kinds of questions. Sometimes they obviously did not read English, as they held our passports upside down to read them! Some articles in our luggage were complete mysteries to them, requiring endless explanations.

We had so many brilliant students who were always curious about America that I am surprised and disappointed not to have run into a single one of them in the US pursuing graduate studies over the years. I am sure many of them must have been here; why didn't we happen to cross paths? I think we connected with only one faculty member who was studying at Brandeis U in Boston. We also heard from Emmanuel Itapson (a professor at Palmer Seminary and a Nigerian living in both countries) about one of our former students, now a bishop in Nigeria. We were so excited that Emmanuel was planning to help us connect, but it never happened.

I greatly enjoyed some of the extra-curricular activities at Crowther. I directed the choir for a few years, which was an absolute delight, as they learned music and sang with great gusto. Another group I greatly enjoyed was the Fellowship of Christian Students. I met with them during their regular meetings as a mentor, but I think I learned more from them than they did from me. They spontaneously sang, prayed, studied the Bible, and testified so eagerly that it was absolutely contagious. Also, I had the privilege of serving as faculty advisor/editor of the school magazine, *The Confluence* (an apt name, since Lokoja is precisely at the confluence of the Niger and Benue Rivers in the middle of the country). I still get out a few old copies occasionally and skim them for memory's sake.

Classroom surprises happened almost daily. Even in our third and final year, when we felt pretty well acclimated and understood the routines, we realized that cross-cultural learning goes on and on. In some ways, that can be good, a constant reminder that cross-cultural communication is a complex process, easily open to misunderstandings.

Speaking another language perfectly is an impossible goal. I picked up on Yoruba words and greetings pretty well, but names still tripped me up. Whenever I called the roll and called on Grace Onishubioyan, the students could not contain their laughter. So I would have them pronounce it for me once more; they would laugh once more. Finally, they had mercy on me and said, "Sir, her name means 'Her father grows sweet yams,' but the way you say it means her father is a witch doctor!" I never mastered the difference. Embarrassing!

Learning English was sometimes difficult for them as well, even for the brightest students. A student would raise his hand and say, "Excuse, Suh, I have to pass your-INE!" At long last, you might finally realize they were trying to pronounce the English word "urine." Or if a student got sick, she might say, "I have to voe-MIT!" and you would soon realize that "vomit" was on the way. English essays were endlessly interesting. No matter the assigned subject, they would often include stories or folklore from their villages. It helped us remember that even though, to us, our students all seemed to be "from here," (Lokoja), many of them were from out of town, sometimes from remote villages far from the city, but they were living with relatives or extended family in Lokoja in order to get an education at Crowther.

On one occasion, two of our students invited us to visit their family in a small village, maybe an hour away. When we arrived, there were numerous people there, some inside and some outside the house. After we had greeted the family, our students took us to a small room, brought us specially prepared dishes, set them before us on a bench, and then walked out and closed the door. We said, "Please come eat with us." They smiled and came to eat with us, apparently not having expected that. This was an example of how deep and ingrained some colonial traditions were.

Time was an ongoing adventure. Time was flexible and approximate, except for the bell that signaled the start or end of class periods. EVENTS, however, were a different matter. Events were huge; elaborate preparation and adherence to tradition were non-negotiable. Speeches were often quite lengthy. It was almost an insult to keep a speech to the allotted time. Details, rabbit trails, and elaboration were the order of the day, even if you were the last speaker in a three-hour ceremony, and there were still songs and presentations to follow. It was a great weariness of the flesh to us time-bound westerners. Pomp and circumstance were ultra-important. Perhaps they had learned all that from the British colonists decades ago, blended with local tribal traditions, of course.

Greetings and introductions were always important. I would tell Naomi I'm going to the bank and will be back by lunch. I soon learned to say I'm going to the bank and I'll be back when I'm back. It totally depended on how many people I needed to meet and greet along the way, how many people were in line at the bank, who happened to be on duty that day, and how many people might ask me for a ride. I remember a particular day when I went to the post office to buy stamps. The post office was open, clerks were at the windows, and I was told, "Sorry, no stamps today; we are getting ready for the holiday tomorrow." So, of course, the next day it really *was* closed, but the day after, when I went back, I was told, "Sorry, we're not selling stamps today; we're still recovering from the holiday yesterday."

Appointments to see dignitaries, authorities, or officials proved to be an art form. You could make and keep an appointment, only to be made to wait endlessly without explanation, or be told after a long wait that something came up and the dignitary had to go away for a few days. Can you come back next week? Travelers often spent the night at our house because the ferry was late, had broken down, or had stopped working — the ferry was the only way across the Niger in our town. Or sometimes the locals would miss their ride because they had too many people to greet or needed to play one more round of a game. We often wondered how a culture and economy such as this could long survive, but survive it did. We were the ones who needed to adjust. If and when we actually *had* time to meet the official we had come to see (perhaps to get a document signed, for example), those visits were often very delightful and informative. Sometimes *we* were the cause of long waits for the people outside waiting after our appointment was over. The dignitaries would offer us pleasant greetings, beverages, and perhaps share interesting stories related to the business at hand.

Missionaries and other ambassadors of goodwill provided us with an endless study in cross-cultural effectiveness. Since we were testing our own call to missions, it seemed important to learn from those who had been at it for some time, to see what worked well and what didn't. We soon discovered that some long-term missionaries seemed comfortably "at home" among their Nigerian neighbors, serving and learning together as fellow humans in God's family. Others seemed most comfortable with the traditional "mission compound" arrangement, in which missionary families lived inside a walled community of cottages, with amenities not always available to their Nigerian neighbors. Sometimes a compound felt like a Little America. Some of us in MCC's TAP program lived among Nigerian neighbors in houses provided by the school, as we did in Lokoja. Other TAP-ers lived among missionaries in mission compounds. At our annual TAP retreats, we compared stories, sometimes with laughter, sometimes with tears.

Some TAP-ers were told by the missionaries not to eat with or give rides to Nigerians, as their food was not safe to eat and giving rides would create dependency. Sometimes, a TAP teacher would transport a seriously ill Nigerian to the hospital on the back of a Honda motorcycle because the missionary would not provide a ride in their car. Obviously, such experiences would create conflicts between missionaries and TAP teachers on the compound or at the mission school. Navigating these conflicting perspectives was an ongoing challenge.

Paul and Caroline Gross, Plymouth Brethren missionaries across the river in Igalaland, provided an exact opposite example. We loved spending time with them, visiting their churches, and observing how lovingly their family and their Nigerian neighbors lived, worked, and worshiped together. Paul's parents had been missionaries there for many years, so Paul grew up with many Igala friends, spoke the language fluently, and enjoyed sharing life and laughter with them daily. When we traveled around their community with them, we would often sit in the hot van, waiting for Paul to finish talking with neighbors so we could move on to the next stop. At times, he would play Mancala with Nigerians by the river and get so caught up in the game that he missed the ferry, so he would have to wait until the next day to cross to Lokoja. Their network of local churches, schools, and health clinics met in small buildings built with local materials and led by Nigerian elders, pastors, and teachers. Paul and Caroline would simply blend in among them. They sang, prayed, and preached in the local language, and joyfully served God and their neighbors in their daily lives. Years later, when Paul died, we heard that hundreds of people from miles around crowded their home and church before, during, and after the wake and funeral service. He was buried in a local cemetery, not flown back to the US for burial, as was the custom of some mission agencies. Here was one missionary family that clearly left a deep imprint on a large region of Igalaland. We were blessed to observe firsthand what a lifetime of commitment to living and sharing the gospel can do to transform and uplift an entire community.

Introductions, greetings, and farewells were always important, never to be minimized or taken for granted. When introducing someone, it was very important to mention credentials, connections, and backgrounds. When visiting someone's home, there were many "greetings" during the ongoing conversation, such as "Are you well seated?" "How is your health?" "How is the family?" and so on. When leaving, the host would always accompany the guests to the door and even out to the car or down the street before finally parting. These greetings and partings were often accompanied by gifts. Guests often brought gifts; hosts often sent you on your way with gifts. These deep traditions made our American habits of hasty hellos and goodbyes seem shallow and almost frivolous. Perhaps they are.

We attended two different churches in our years in Lokoja. Because we were at an Anglican school, at first we attended the local Anglican church, the only English service in town. The high-church liturgy seemed strange at first, but we appreciated the deep prayers and meaningful homilies, especially by Judge Dandaura, who became a good friend. Later we also attended the local Baptist church, which felt more like what we were used to, but all services were in Yoruba. The jubilant singing, testimonies, and passionate sermons moved and inspired us, even though we sometimes needed translation. The Baptist church gave us complete Yoruba outfits as farewell gifts.

The final farewell for us at the end of our three years is a perfect example. After we said our tearful goodbyes to faculty, students, and friends, the school held a public farewell for us. After some farewell speeches and prayers, the students and faculty lined up on both sides of the school's long driveway as our car made its slow and painful exit, all of us waving and crying until we were out of sight. But that was not the end of it. Reverend Yakubu and several carloads of Baptist church members were waiting to escort us slowly out of town. A few miles down the road, we all pulled off the road under a tree. Everyone got out and formed a big circle for yet another round of prayers, hugs, and farewell blessings. Along with various gifts from school and friends, the church gave both Naomi and me complete, hand-sewn and embroidered Yoruba outfits to treasure and wear whenever we needed to feel Nigeria's enveloping love again. Finally, we slowly began the long road trip toward Lagos, the first leg of our journey back home. Our hearts were full of joy and sadness at the same time, knowing we would likely never see these dear friends again in our lifetimes. What amazing love and hospitality we will treasure forever!

Our three-year commitment to TAP in Nigeria with Mennonite Central Committee included the proviso that MCC would pay all our travel costs and a monthly stipend to cover our living expenses. All personal expenses were ours to cover. This meant MCC was ready to pay for our flight home, but any sightseeing side trips would be our personal expense. MCC would fly us from Lagos to London, then on to New York. But we wanted to see Europe on our way home, so we arranged with MCC to fly us to Rome, then provide us with a Eurail Pass from

Rome to Amsterdam by rail, a short flight to London, and then on to New York. Our leisurely week of traveling through Europe was a welcome respite after three hot years in the tropics. We saw beautiful scenery with a few key stops along the way. While we could have wished for more time and more stops, it was a blessing to see Europe on the ground and not only through an airplane window.

We spent a night or two in Rome, visited the Vatican, then took a train to Pisa, where we got off and took a taxi to Miselia/Carrara, Italy, near the marble mountain from which Michaelangelo got most of the marble for his sculptures. We spent a few days with the Giuseppi Lazarini family, whom we had met in Lokoja. They were marble dealers living in a village where even the curbs along the street were made of marble! We spent several days with them, ate sumptuous meals, and toured the marble quarry on the mountain, feeling like royalty in their spacious home. We also saw the Leaning Tower of Pisa, but it was closed for repairs, so we could not go up into it.

Back on the train, we journeyed north through Italy and into Switzerland, stopping briefly in Zurich to see where the Anabaptist movement began, where we were startled to run into three friends from back home! Three young ladies from the United Bethel church were on a tour, and we just happened to meet them in our brief stopover. After reboarding the train, we made our way through the Alps and northward through Germany, which included a ride along the Rhine and a stopover in Cologne. I was intrigued by the various accents detected across Germany, some of which sounded almost like the Plain City, Pennsylvania German of my youth. I would have loved to trace my roots back to my ancestors' town or village, but alas! I don't know where that is, nor did we have time. We continued to Amsterdam by train, where we spent a night with my cousin, Ralph Mast, who was living in Amsterdam, and gave us a quick tour. A rare visit and way too short. Then it was a short plane ride to London, where we spent a few days with a friend we had met in Port Harcourt, Nigeria, near the end of the war. We got to stay with real Londoners and got a first-hand look at the city through British eyes. What a wonderful way to end our European excursion! Along the way, we met many interesting people, with varying degrees of success in translating and communicating nonverbally with those who spoke little or no English. Weary, but happy, we were ready for our flight back to New York.

CHAPTER 9

Return to America

When we returned to Ohio from Nigeria early in the fall of 1970, we faced a few immediate challenges: finding a place to live and finding jobs to make living there affordable, not to mention a car for travel, adjusting back to temperate climates, and deciding in what community to settle for the time being. The only thing Naomi and I were both sure of was that God was calling us to return to work in the cities of America rather than pursue a lifetime of mission work in Africa. While the needs in Africa were great, in Nigeria we lived among many gifted and dedicated Christians who were working effectively to meet them. Our faith was nurtured by vibrant faith communities. While we were addressing a temporary teacher shortage, Nigeria was training a new generation of educators to meet that need.

Meanwhile, the cities of America were burning, leaders were being assassinated, most notably Martin Luther King and Robert F. Kennedy, and anti-war and other protests were surging across the country. Social and racial unrest was widespread, threatening the peace and welfare of the country, especially in the cities. Slowly but surely, Naomi and I both felt God calling us to return to the US, to "seek the welfare of the city," as the Bible puts it in Jeremiah 29:7. So our time in Nigeria was extremely valuable, equipping us for a lifetime of cross-cultural urban ministry, even though our call was gradually redirected back to America. Now we needed to decide which American city or cities and what kind of "work" we were to pursue.

Since we both had earned degrees in secondary English education and teaching certificates in Ohio, it seemed reasonable to start there. Sure enough, I was able to secure a job teaching English at East High School in Columbus, right back in the city where we had earned our degrees and certificates. East High seemed like a good choice, as it was a predominantly African-American school, and perhaps our having lived in an African country would give us some credibility within the Black community in the city. We could also attend Burnside Mennonite Church, the church we had attended in a small Black community on the west side of the city while we were students at Ohio State. Additionally, we were able to secure an apartment in the same building on North High Street where we had lived before going to Nigeria. Perfect!

Burnside Mennonite Church was a dynamic small church on the edge of Columbus in a Black neighborhood, surrounded by White communities on all sides. Naomi's father, Mark Peachey, was their bishop while they were part of the Conservative Mennonite Conference, and Paul Yutzy from Plain City was the pastor for years. Eugene Norris, a young leader in the church, formed a choir, "The Mennonaires," a pioneer among Black Gospel choirs arising in a few Mennonite communities. Norris, who taught himself to play the piano, was a gifted singer and musician. In 1972, the Minority Ministries Council of the Mennonite Church recorded an album titled *Praises* with the choir. It was a ground-breaking recording as the Mennonite Church was wrestling with how to include minority voices in the life and structures of the church.

East High School was a large school in the heart of the Black community on the city's east side. It had a very smart African-American principal, an experienced white assistant principal, and a multicultural faculty of committed, experienced teachers who had learned to navigate the less-than-ideal realities of inner-city schools. It proved to be an excellent setting for further experience in cross-cultural urban ministry and service. A fine "re-entry" into American society for us.

Teaching English at a large inner-city high school proved challenging. While most classes had a committed core of diligent students who consistently did classwork and homework with solid support from home, others were not very motivated to learn. On most days, dozens of students were absent, which meant they often missed multiple days of learning and consequently struggled to keep up with their classwork. Grades suffered. Morale sagged. Many students were not highly motivated to learn, especially when it came to "standard" English. One student said, "My mom would kill me if I talked like this at home!" African American street language, often referred to as "Ebonics," proved to be just as much of their language as Pidgin English in Nigeria or Pennsylvania Dutch in Plain City. The city's street language included many new slang terms that were constantly evolving. What was once "cool" or "hip" was now "bad" or "dope." A high compliment from a student might be, "Mr. Miller, those are some bad threads!" referring positively to an outfit I was wearing.

Unless I connected my classroom lessons to my students' immediate life experiences, I was an outsider to them. One result was that we finally bought a TV so that I could watch some of the popular shows my students were talking about and relate them to our stories or exercises in our English textbooks. We also wanted to immerse ourselves in urban Black culture, to know what mattered to my students at home, at church, and on the street. Unless teaching is relevant to real-life experiences, it becomes merely an academic exercise. It raises the familiar cry from students, "Why do I have to learn this stuff? I'm never going to use any of it in my life." It's a fair question. Learning must have meaning in life, or it can feel tedious and irrelevant. Of course, meaningful, relevant learning may also seem boring at times.

As I mentioned earlier, Mr. Gibbs, our Black principal, was a very wise man. He knew his audience and understood his context. One day, there was going to be a protest downtown at the police station, I believe, mostly by Black people about a perceived injustice, no doubt a familiar and legitimate complaint, as we had just come through the social upheaval of the 60's. Soon after the school day had begun, Mr. Gibbs' voice came over the PA system, saying something like this, "I'm very disappointed in our fine students at East High School. Some of you are coming to ask if you can be excused from school to go downtown and join the protest. I was down there myself bright and early, before school, and thought I would see you there! But instead, you want to miss a day of your very important education, even though you should have joined me early and then come to class. You are not excused! Classes will continue as normal. I hope you will do better next time and keep your priorities straight." Wow, what could they say to that? Mr. Gibbs clearly believed the protest was a worthy cause, but not at the expense of life-long learning. He turned their complaint into a lesson they did not soon forget.

Principal Gibbs seemed to have organized an informal network of "private eyes," students he could count on to alert him to potential troublemakers or dissatisfied groups in the student body. He could then cleverly subvert or prevent potential uprisings by calling an impromptu pep rally in the auditorium and staging a celebration instead. No one will ever know how many school crises he averted by always being a step ahead of the students–and perhaps even ahead of the teachers! When Principal Gibbs spoke, students and staff listened. He was a respected head of school, surrounded by a gifted multicultural team of assistants. He ran a tight ship, providing a quality education for an underserved population in the city.

Several delightful discoveries awaited me at East High. A group of seasoned Christian teachers gathered weekly over lunch to share stories, pray, and encourage one another. I gladly accepted their invitation to join the group. It was wonderful to talk with fellow believers as I learned to cope and teach effectively at a large inner-city high school. Also, a student-led gospel choir filled the halls with heavenly praise after school on many days. What joy! You could tell that the students were pouring their entire being into their worship, singing at the top of their lungs as they clapped, swayed, stomped, and cheered one another on in their faith journeys. What a wonderful gift they were to the school! I have since learned that such choirs are not uncommon in public city schools, especially in black and brown communities. Extracurriculars provide ample opportunities to express faith and culture.

A significant challenge for me was maintaining order and discipline in the classroom. With hundreds of students in a large multi-story building, it was inevitable that chaos and noise would often fill the hallways before and after school, between classes, during assemblies, and during any activities outside of class. When students came into my classroom, after all the jostling and noise in the hall, they weren't necessarily ready or eager for an English lesson. It took time for all to find their seats, settle down, and get ready for class. Depending on the time of day, home situation, age, and health, my students might be hungry, sleepy, or otherwise unready to learn. Getting everyone's attention, focusing on the lesson of the day, and providing some real and relevant learning–these are daily, hourly challenges for every teacher, every day, in every school everywhere. At East High School, I needed help from my English Department chair and other veteran teachers to find my footing in this new world, very different from any previous classroom settings I had experienced.

I made many adjustments to my teaching style to better communicate with my students. I watched TV shows I had heard about so I could use parallels or draw contrasts in my lessons, especially when teaching literature. I watched the news and read the *Columbus Dispatch* so I could relate my lessons to real events in various neighborhoods of the city. I learned that to get my students' attention, I would have to use a sharper, louder tone and speak with a stern, commanding voice. I began to hear myself sometimes almost shouting commands at my students. Sometimes I went home and looked in the mirror, wondering who I was becoming. My "home voice" and "school voice" were two different "dialects" of the same language. I grew up in a restrained, non-assertive culture; East High was in a more assertive one, where I had to learn to speak up and command attention to be heard. That was not easy for me, as it did not seem "natural" for me. Adaptability is a must in cross-cultural communication, but it gets complicated when your assignment is to teach "proper" English in the classroom. There is formal and informal usage, "standard" and colloquial expression, written and spoken parlance, in addition to local dialects. A tall order for students and teachers alike.

Having Ms. Cooley in the classroom next to mine was a plus. An African American with many years of teaching experience, she had earned the respect of the students. She was a straight shooter, a no-nonsense teacher with a heart. She wanted students to succeed, but knew they needed to take their studies seriously and not mess around. Any students who gave me any trouble would straighten right up when Ms. Cooley appeared. The most important talk I ever heard on adoption was delivered by Ms. Cooley to a student who was feeling sorry for himself because he was adopted. She sat him down and said, "Now you listen to me..." and proceeded to outline in detail how he had advantages above many others because he was chosen, loved, and supported by caring people who wanted him in their home, which was more than some other students might be able to say. He sobered right up, sat up straight, wiped the frown off his face, and I don't think I ever heard him complain after that. Great teachers teach more than simply the material in their lesson plans.

While some teachers sat in the teachers' lounge and bemoaned having to "go face the brats" in the next class period, many others were dedicated to their calling and would not give up, no matter how challenging some school years were. I remember Mrs. White, a white woman with very white hair, who had tried to retire several times, but always came back. She just loved her students too much to stop teaching. She kept on teaching as long as they would hire her, and the students loved her. Public schools have many unsung heroes like Mrs. White.

The most important event during my two years of teaching at East High was the birth of Janelle, our oldest daughter. It happened on a Monday in September 1971. I called in to the school to say our first baby was on the way, and I had to miss school to take Naomi to the hospital. Of course, I had warned the school that it could happen at any given moment. It was an eventful day. I was not allowed into the actual birthing room, but I stayed with Naomi as long as they would allow. After Janelle was born, the whole world changed. Becoming a parent is momentous beyond words. Naomi and I repeatedly looked at that precious little bundle of joy and tried to comprehend the incredible truth that Janelle was somehow a combination of both of us. She was adorable and cute, making the most amazing cooing sounds along with healthy cries. Even her messy diapers seemed cute at first. We were responsible for bringing her into this world, and now we were also responsible for taking care of her, making sure she remained healthy. Who could be truly prepared for such a daunting task? It is often said that children do not come with an instruction manual. How true! Even if they did, no two children are alike, so no one edition of such a manual would apply equally to each new child. Of course, the Creator of Life has left us a "Life Manual," the Bible, which is full of wisdom to apply in all life cases, including parenting. It is full of parenting models, good and bad.

We lived only 20 miles from Plain City, so our extended family and friends came to see this new baby and the new parents, which was appreciated. Nevertheless, we also treasured time alone just to get used to being a family. One of my sisters came to stay with us for the first week to help with household chores as we adjusted to having a baby in the family. Janelle was a healthy and responsive little baby. Her coos and smiles brought oceans of new joy into our lives. As she grew, we took her to church, took her along to events in Plain City, and doted on her with all the love and energy we could muster.

At age 29, this was my tenth straight year of teaching, three of them in the tropics of West Africa, followed by two in an inner-city high school. These all began taking their toll. With the added duties of parenthood and some responsibilities at church, I began to feel exhausted and wondered if I might be at risk of burnout. I wished for a "sabbatical," with time to study the Bible and find refreshment for my soul. But how could we afford such a "luxury" at this point in our lives?

God apparently heard our inner groanings, because at some point, Naomi's father, Mark Peachey, mentioned that Richard and Jewel Showalter were helping to start an intentional Christian community in Harrisonburg, VA. He suggested we might consider joining them. That was a bold new idea! We prayed, considered, talked with the Showalters, and decided to join them. The fall of 1972 found us packing our things into a U-Haul truck and heading for Harrisonburg to attend Eastern Mennonite Seminary and to live with the Showalters and others in a new intentional Christian community they were forming.

I got the one year of Bible study I had prayed for, plus a whole lot more. One year became two, two became three, and we lived with a group of other Christians in a new intentional community, eventually named "The Gemeinschaft." They had covenanted to share time, money, and resources, enabling some to study and/or serve while others worked and combined their earnings to support the group. That freed me up to take classes and also work part-time. Those three years became pivotal in preparing us for the future.

Enrolling at Eastern Mennonite Seminary (EMS) was exhilarating. I had not really considered seminary before, as I envisioned myself being a lifelong educator, not a pastor. I knew that seminaries offered tracks other than preparation for pastoral ministry, but I had not given them serious thought. (While I was teaching at East High School, I took some graduate-level English courses at Ohio State, thinking that was the additional training that would be most useful.) Since I thought I would only have one year for spiritual refreshment at EMS, I chose the biblical courses that looked most interesting to me. As I bought the required textbooks, notebooks, and other supplies, I got really excited about going back to school–especially grad school–with a focus on Bible and faith development. I got a fresh burst of enthusiasm. I could get my spirit refreshed instead of pouring my emotional energies into developing other people. What a gift!

Going to class, studying the Bible, memorizing Greek and Hebrew, writing papers, taking exams–all of this actually energized me. While some of my classmates were groaning about all the coursework and needing more education to achieve their career goals, I was exhilarated by the opportunity. I knew from experience in "the real world" that every bit of relevant learning can be an invaluable asset. I began to realize that lifelong learning was a key component of teaching and leading. I was eager to learn more about God, about the Bible, about life.

Several other unexpected blessings made those three seminary years especially memorable: Naomi's parents and brother joined us for one of those years, and I got to join the seminary chorus (choir). Mark Peachey, Naomi's father, was granted a mini-sabbatical from Rosedale Mennonite Missions, so Mark and Fannie Peachey moved to Harrison-burg, where Mark took seminary courses for one year. He and I took a class or two together (I remember an Old Testament class on Jeremiah in particular), and enjoyed being on campus together. Naomi's brother Titus had just returned from three years in Vietnam and decided to join us at EMC for a year as well. So Naomi's entire family (except for her sister Nona and family) was with us for that very special year, all on the same college campus.

Mark and I enjoyed singing with the seminary chorus and were privileged to experience a most memorable road trip that winter. Being stranded in a blizzard for six hours on the Pennsylvania Turnpike made it more memorable than usual. On the trip, we sang our hearts out at various churches across several states and also poured a lot of energy into a short play included in our chorus program. The play was a re-enactment of the trial of Michael Sattler, an early leader and martyr in the Anabaptist movement in Switzerland. It was part of our commemoration of the 450th anniversary of the birth of Anabaptism. As I played the part of Sattler, I got to experience what it must have felt like to be tried as a traitor to one's faith, being harshly accused by the judge and others in the courtroom, and ultimately sentenced to death (https://mennonitelife.catalogaccess.com/archives/52863). It was a visceral reminder to all of us of the high price our spiritual foreparents often paid in defending their faith, and how many believers around the world today still face fierce persecution for their faith. It made our seminary coursework seem all the more valuable and worth struggling through. We needed a deep grounding for our faith.

Seminary student (Freeman Miller) as Michael Sattler, defends his beliefs before a partial judge (Sam Wenger) in a dramatic sketch, "The Trial of Michael Sattler" presented by the EMS chorus.

My training as an English teacher served me well. I found myself editing campus newspapers from Plainview School in Ohio to Crowther Memorial College in Nigeria to Eastern Mennonite Seminary in Virginia to Diamond Street Mennonite Church in Philadelphia.

Living at The Gemeinschaft (German for "community") was an education in itself. We joined several other young families and single adults who had pledged to live together as an expression of the church, similar to the one outlined in Acts 2 and Acts 4, where they had "all things in common and no one was in need." We pooled our possessions, time, and talents to live, work, eat, play, and worship together in Park View, a small suburb on the edge of the city of Harrisonburg, near the campus of Eastern Mennonite College (now University) and Seminary

Eventually, we bought and renovated a huge old house on a hill overlooking the campus. We all moved into that big house together. We were not exactly a "city on a hill," as Jesus put it, but we wanted to try a different way of being church together, modeled after the early church in the New Testament. Married couples had their own bedrooms, while single young adults shared rooms arranged like college dorm rooms, men and women seperately. Because Naomi and I had children, we had our own small apartment on the second floor. The entire community ate one common meal together around a long table each evening, taking turns cooking and washing dishes, while other meals were "on your own." Keeping the common kitchen, dining room, and large living room clean was a shared task, plotted out on a posted schedule. We used each other's cars, appliances, tools, and living room furniture. Once a week, we had common worship together; some of us were also members at local churches, attending Sunday services there. At that time, there were fourteen of us living together at the Gemeinschaft. Occasionally, local friends would join us for a meal or fellowship. Here is an early photo of our group:

Some of us worked full-time, some part-time; others studied or taught; some went to school and worked part-time (I was one of those). By pooling our incomes and other resources, we could free up more options and possibilities for everyone. Combining finances was a tricky business. Some with sizable incomes put their paychecks into the same bank account as those with little or nothing to share. This required humility and trust. Each member received a small monthly allowance to buy toothpaste and other personal effects, but all other spending was from the common purse. Weekly grocery shopping was also on the posted schedule. Some of us had cars, some had bikes, and some had no vehicles at all. In our case, since we had very little money to contribute, aside from my part-time job selling potato chips, we made our living room furniture, washer and dryer, our car, and canned goods available for community use. We were also on the community schedule to take our turns cooking, doing dishes, cleaning, grocery shopping, doing yard work, and attending community business and worship meetings, just like everyone else.

Needless to say, this unusual arrangement required adjustments to daily living that called into question all previous habits and practices. What decisions are mine alone, and which do I need to make as part of a group process? Who decides on mealtimes, bedtimes, quiet times–and all other times? Do we have curfews? Who chooses what food to buy and cook? Are single members automatically free babysitters? What about levels of decor and decorum? What kinds of music could we play and how loudly? Whose child-rearing policies would we follow? Whose worship preferences would prevail at our common worship times? Who could invite guests to dinner, how often, and how many? Thorny, complex issues all, in an individualistic culture such as America.

To reach a common mind on these many issues, we held weekly business meetings to pray, discuss, and make group decisions. Those were very interesting times! Let me offer a few examples. I remember one touchy topic for those who did grocery shopping and cooking: how much ice cream should we keep in the freezer, and who was allowed to eat it? Some were used to eating ice cream whenever they felt like it; others thought it a luxury to be enjoyed only at special occasions. We finally resolved the issue by saying the weekly grocery shoppers would buy two gallons of ice cream, one marked "Free for all," and the other, "save for dinner time only." When the one "free for all" gallon was gone, that was it. Those planning and cooking the evening meals would decide on when to eat the other gallon as dessert. Another difficult question was whether cooking included cleanup. Some thought that if they cooked, others should clean the oven, stove, and kitchen. We finally decided cooking and cleanup were one single operation, so do your common duty. Vegetarians and vegans also posed a challenge for carnivores. I don't quite remember how we resolved that one. I believe one solution was to observe "Meatless Mondays."

We added something very special of our own during our second year at The Gemeinschaft: a new baby! Our second daughter, Rhonda, was born in October of that year. What a joy to bring home another baby girl, a precious new gift from God! This new bundle of joy brought us endless delight, along with all the necessary adjustments, of course. Janelle was so happy to have a baby sister, although she now had to share her parents' attention, of course. She wasn't always sure whether to treat her like a miniature human or a doll. I now had to juggle even more family time with studying for classes, driving the potato chip truck, teaching Sunday School, and other duties at church. I could have used a few months' paternity leave, if such a thing had existed, but all I got was two "D's" in Greek class, according to Naomi's journal jottings. But it was all worth it! Here is a photo of Janelle feeding Rhonda with a bottle:

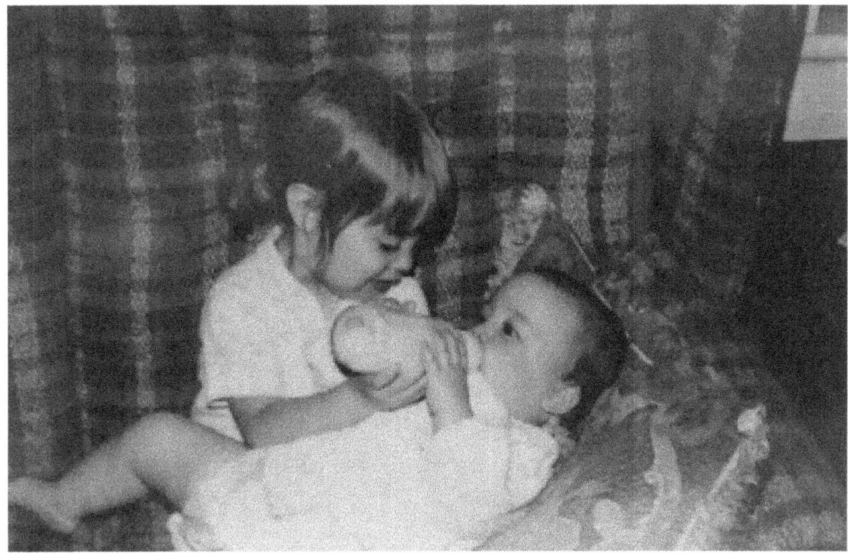

Our baby girl brought joy not only to our little family but to the entire Gemeinschaft family. Not every newborn gets to be admired, cuddled, and fussed over by fourteen loving adults all living under one roof! Everyone wanted a turn holding or otherwise attending to this baby girl. But a newborn was added to the community, bringing new challenges. Who gets to hold the new baby? When? How often? What do we do when nighttime crying disturbs the sleep of others in the house? Are all the adults in the group automatic free babysitters? Do the birth parents get excused from some community commitments because of new responsibilities? Nothing is simple when living in an intentional community. Adjustments had to be made along the way, but blessings were shared as well. Every growing "family" has its own growing pains. Our nuclear family fit into the Gemeinschaft for a few years, but by the third year we moved into an apartment nearby, still part of the Gemeinschaft but not full members. Before moving on, let me describe a few more aspects of group dynamics in living together as an intentional community, which help explain our decision to move into our own apartment.

As mentioned above, group decisions did not always come easily. One question was how to outfit the common living room. Some of us brought living room furniture; others had none. The large living room required more than one sofa and an easy chair, of course. People who heard about The Gemeinschaft wanted to contribute furniture and furnishings to help us get established. But what if the sofas, drapes, and rugs didn't all match? Some of us thought that living the simple, frugal life meant we should accept all donations without question or debate. Others thought we needed an inviting, pleasant space for entertaining guests and providing a reflective worship space, which meant decor and decorum were important community attributes. During the first few years, some members moved on, and others joined us, so the common areas changed a bit over time to accommodate shared contributions and concerns. Patterns shifted while central commitments remained. Living "in community" certainly provided rich opportunities for reflection on what really matters in life. Becoming sensitive to the needs of others requires practice and intentionality, especially in a self-centered society like America.

A more contentious issue was the matter of worship style. Our weekly worship was rather informal at first, featuring singing, testimonies, prayer, and short devotional meditations by community members. Singing from Mennonite hymnbooks came naturally to most of us. For the less-initiated, four-part acapella singing seemed unusual and culturally rich at first, but blending in and harmonizing took time and practice. Sometimes guitars or other instruments were added. Often, we included vigorous discussion or debate, depending on the topic or text at hand. Sometimes we invited a guest speaker, which was not too difficult, given the proximity to several local colleges and churches. Stimulating debates were common.

All of this changed when several Quakers joined the community. At first, they introduced a few Quaker traditions, such as silent prayer before the common evening meal together. They explained that silent, inner prayer was deeper and richer than praying aloud as a group. Also, since prayer should be "without ceasing," there should be no "Amen" at the end of the prayer; instead, someone simply squeezed a neighbor's hand, which started a chain reaction around the circle, and the eating and talking began (although prayers might still be silently ascending heavenward during the meal). So that became the new tradition. It was simple and easy; no one needed to be appointed to lead in prayer, which some were reluctant to do anyway. Nevertheless, questions remained. Was this the only or best way to pray? What if someone wanted to pray out loud? How did we offer group prayers for people with special needs, both locally and globally? How did we express personal needs without praying for each other?

Later, the Quakers persuaded the group to try a few "unprogrammed" (silent) worship services in the Quaker style. There was to be deep, contemplative silence for fifteen minutes, after which someone could speak, if moved by the Spirit. Then, more silence until someone else was moved to speak. If no one else felt moved to speak, after an hour of silence and deep listening, the designated leader would shake hands with someone nearby; everyone would shake hands, and the meeting was over. Those of us used to Mennonite worship did not adjust easily, as we were accustomed to vigorous singing, preaching, discussion, and prayer. The somber silence did not quite satisfy us, but we gradually adjusted to this new "normal." No singing, no sermons, no amens.

The Quaker influence was strong, as the two Friends among us had deep convictions about this style of living, working, and worshiping. Eventually, this became the regular worship pattern each week, which again required little planning. But those of us who wanted singing, guest speakers, group discussions, and open prayers began to lose out. Some of us joined the weekly Gemeinschaft worship, but also worshiped with a local church on Sundays. This arrangement worked rather well until the community members finally decided that everyone must join the weekly Gemeinschaft worship only, being entirely committed to the group rather than holding membership in two "churches." This was a painful moment for us. Eventually, our family moved into a nearby apartment and continued our involvement with Community Mennonite Church, which I had helped to plant, and which we had attended all along. We maintained a loose relationship with the Gemeinschaft but were not full members. It was a difficult decision, as we had formed deep relationships with others in the group. The needs of our daughters, along with our call to ministry in a large American city, were pulling us away, and I was about to graduate from seminary.

Seminary graduation also brought Community Mennonite Church to a decision point. Owen Burkholder and I were the two seminarians assigned to lead this young church plant (as part of our fieldwork assignment) under the supervision of several seminary professors, including Myron Augsburger, the college and seminary's president. We had both given a lot of time, thought, prayer, and energy to launching this new church in Harrisonburg, helping to shape its vision, culture, and structure. It was doing well, and people were joining and experimenting with new ways to reach urban neighborhoods with the gospel. Members were divided into "modules" (small groups), worship styles were flexible, and we recommitted to the membership covenant every year on a recommitment Sunday. This church took seriously its task of making the Anabaptist vision real and relational in a contemporary urban context. We had something fresh, genuine, and alive. We were beginning to feel like family. This was what the church should be like!

But now Owen and I were both about to graduate with Master of Divinity degrees after three good years in seminary, which had equipped us for church leadership. We both needed full-time employment to support our young families. Community Mennonite Church could only afford to support one pastor half-time at this point, which presented a dilemma for Owen, me, and our families. The church made it clear that they loved us both and wished they could keep us both on as co-pastors, but that was unrealistic. Meanwhile, Owen and I had each received invitations to pastor churches in other cities and needed to make some important decisions about our long-term ministry plans. Community Mennonite Church began meeting to pray and discuss various possibilities for the church and for the two of us church-planting couples.

Earlier in the semester, I met with representatives from various conferences or mission boards who were recruiting pastors for churches in urban locations. Naomi and I were praying for God to direct us to the city and church that matched our sense of call. One invitation in particular resonated with us: the call from Diamond Street Mennonite Church in Philadelphia. Bishop Luke Stoltzfus of the Philadelphia District and Chester Wenger, Director of Home Ministries for Eastern Mennonite Missions, met with me at the seminary and explained that this young church in the heart of a large African American community in North Philadelphia was without a lead pastor. They were looking for someone to lead the multicultural congregation in its efforts to grow and explore new ways to reach its neighbors with the Good News of Christ. As we learned more specific details about this church, its location, and vision, we began to feel drawn to Philadelphia. Owen and

Ruth Ann Burkholder were likewise considering various options and invitations, deliberating where God might be calling them.

After prayer and discernment, we decided that it seemed good to our young urban church and to both of us couples: Naomi and I would follow our call to serve Diamond Street Mennonite Church in Philadelphia. Owen and Ruth Ann would stay to pastor CMC at least for the time being, as the church pondered long-term arrangements. Even though Owen and Ruth Ann needed full-time employment, Owen agreed to serve as a half-time pastor, at least for the moment, trusting God to fill their financial needs. This decision freed up the church and the two of us couples to begin planning our futures.

Now it was time for Naomi and me to wrap up this leg of our journey and prepare for the next. What was originally intended as a one-year spiritual refresher for me turned into a three-year, full-blown seminary education. God was calling us to pastor a church in the heart of North Philadelphia, America's fifth-largest city at that time. Our call to urban America finally had a specific name and place. As we began packing up to move and making our rounds of farewells, we realized how many wonderful friends we had made and how difficult it would be to separate from them geographically. The church sent us off with their blessing and support. Our tight-knit seminary class said our tearful goodbyes, just as every graduating class always must. Our friends at the Gemeinschaft and in Harrisonburg wished us well, even though parting was painful. In the spring of 1975, our little family was headed north with all our belongings packed into our little blue VW bug and a U-Haul truck. A new chapter awaited us, and we were eager to see what the future would hold.

CHAPTER 10

Move to Philadelphia

On June 6, 1975 we drove our U-Haul truck and little blue VW "beetle" into Philadelphia. When we pulled up in front of 1936 E. York Street and began to unload, we knew we had just taken one gigantic step as a tiny family--with a truckload of battered and happily lived-in belongings, two little girls, ages 1 and 3, and a few excited and nervous parents, about to begin a whole new life in the City of Brotherly Love.

I remember the first moments vividly. It was a sunny spring day as we made our way through the streets of a strange new big city, bustling and full of life, with two million residents, of whom we had met a total of maybe ten. It is fair to say that we personally knew only two: Luke and Miriam Stoltzfus, who were there at our new house when we arrived. As I recall, they had also arranged for Don and Dorothy Schmucker, as well as Barbara Baynard, to be there to welcome us and help move our things into the three-story row house in the Kensington section of the city. They made us feel welcome, fed us lunch, and gave us some timely tips on living in the inner city. They were all part of Diamond Street Mennonite Church, the church I was called to pastor.

We soon met the Fischetti family next door and the Spano family two doors down. The house on the other side of us was vacant. Our house was a typical Philadelphia rowhouse, with a solid brick front wall that connected all the houses tightly, and flat roofs joined on top.

Backyards touched, with a chain-link fence separating them, so it was easy to talk to your neighbors over the backyard fence or on your steps (called "stoops" in Philly) out front. We soon learned some of the benefits of living in a rowhouse in a big city. Frost's famous line, "Good fences make good neighbors," comes to mind.

Both families had lived there for years, so they were very helpful in orienting us to the neighborhood. The Fischetti family, with only a wall between us, was everything we could ask for in next-door neighbors. "Mother Carlson," the grandmother, was a wonderful neighbor, always cheerful and ready to help or give advice. So were Mr. and Mrs. Fischetti and their two teenage daughters. Their daughters and ours became good friends. They were excellent babysitters. We were so grateful to have such wonderful neighbors. They were happy to provide any advice we needed about our house, our block, or our city.

The Spano family owned a trash-collecting business, keeping their trucks and other equipment in a large fenced-in lot across the street. They were a well-established family-owned business that helped keep our city clean. We would see their trucks collecting trash all around the city. They also had a few watchdogs keeping an eye on their equipment across the street, so the dogs helped keep our neighborhood safe. The dogs would also alert us whenever a fire truck siren sounded nearby, or the El train wheels screeched around the curve at the end of our block. Yes, the city can be a noisy place at times, but some of the noises become familiar with time, and even provide a sense of security, a sense that things are running as planned. For people moving into the city, this is an adjustment. The reverse is also true: people moving from the city to the suburbs or countryside may feel isolated. Nighttime can be especially scary for them when they are not surrounded by people, light, and comforting noises.

Here is a photo of our new rowhome, with Naomi sitting with the girls on our stoop under the small tree. Fischetti and Spano homes to the right of the tree.

A very exciting detail of our new home was the 15 x 40-foot fenced-in backyard with a real rose garden, green grass, and room for swings, a sandbox, and a roofed-in patio! Wow, our own little private "park" in the middle of the inner city! The vacant house next door had a lush backyard as well, with a cherry tree whose branches hung over the fence, promising fruitful summers. It turns out that our little girls and their friends would have hours of fun in that backyard, with memories we will treasure forever. So much for the stereotype that says inner-city children never see a tree or a blade of grass! Or the familiar misnomer of the city as a "concrete jungle." There is much beauty in the city if you pay attention and know where to look. Even cracks in the sidewalk can spring a beautiful spray of flowers.

We came to Philly with the conviction that urban churches and their pastors are most effective when they live in the neighborhood where they worship, where they can live out the gospel among the neighbors surrounding the church. We thought we wanted to live in the area where Diamond Street Mennonite Church was located, but our bishop and mission board wisely suggested that we move temporarily into a vacant house that Eastern Mennonite Missions (EMM) had inherited and owned. This turned out to be a good idea, as we could live in our new city for a while before deciding where to live permanently.

It was also a good learning experience to live and shop in a low-income, mostly White neighborhood while crossing over almost daily into a low-income, mostly Black one. Most residents in each community could not imagine living in the other. 1936 E. York Street and 1814 W. Diamond Street were only 15 minutes apart by car, but might as well have been two different countries separated by an ocean named Front Street. Living in those separate worlds for five years proved to be an invaluable lesson in cross-cultural relationships and interethnic misperceptions.

These are my vivid first impressions of the city where we would spend over fifty years of family life. That little backyard on York Street helped create our favorite metaphor for the urban church: God's People Garden. We were here to help cultivate God's People Garden.

It has been important to keep our evolving impressions of city life in context, holding up our real-life experiences against the backdrop of William Penn's vision of "a greene countrie towne" when he drew up his plans for Philadelphia. I still sometimes read his "Prayer for Philadelphia," mounted as a bronze plaque on the outside wall of City Hall. It is clear that a founding vision often has a lasting impact on organizations, cities, or nations. It is equally clear that no vision is ever perfectly realized if it involves imperfect human beings. While many socioeconomic issues challenge our great city—as in most large cities—it is amazing how many things of beauty abound and surprise us in the City of Brotherly Love, the longer we live here. Penn's original vision continues to hold power and promise.

Kensington — the neighborhood where we first lived — is one of many neighborhoods that make up the City of Brotherly Love. The locals often mock that nickname, dubbing it the City of Brotherly Shove, which makes sense when one realizes how seriously the neighborhoods have defined themselves over time and how fiercely they defend themselves and their "turf" against equally loyal and proud neighboring communities. Even today, when you buy a SEPTA transit map, the dozens of little neighborhoods making up this great city are still named in blue letters, just like counties on state road maps. While there are no official boundaries and no firm lists or numbers of neighborhoods, the fact that Philadelphia is a "city of neighborhoods" is undisputed.

Two striking early memories of Kensington are the El trains and the shopping strip under the El tracks, just two blocks from our house. Day and night, the noisy trains on the Market-Frankford SEPTA subway/elevated line rumbled through the neighborhood, stopping at the York-Dauphin station, picking up and dropping off hundreds of commuters on the way to or from work or play. It became the easiest, fastest way to the heart of Center City, now immediately accessible to us for a simple subway token. Tokens probably cost 35 cents at the time; now they cost $2.50. The El was convenient for going to concerts, visiting museums, eating at downtown restaurants, or attending Phillies games without worrying about traffic or parking. It was also a fun way to show our city to visitors from out of town.

I remember well taking Mom and Dad on an El train ride downtown during one of their earliest visits, and wondering how my Amish-farmer parents would do on the noisy, crowded, jerky El train. Mom grabbed hold of one of the metal bars to steady herself as she moved to an empty seat. I thought my shy country mother would feel so out of place and want to get off this train as soon as possible. To my utter surprise, she said, "Oh, this is how I would travel if I lived here!" I guess it seemed much safer and simpler than navigating the streets in a car. I wish I could remember more about that trip. Where did we go? What did we see? What else did Mom and Dad say? Did we buy them cheesesteaks or soft pretzels? Did we eat at the popular restaurant on the ninth floor of the old Wanamaker department store?

The line of stores right under the El tracks at Front and York became a favorite shopping strip for things we needed quickly when we didn't have time to drive to a supermarket or shopping center. That strip defied definition, as in a two-block stretch, one could find every type of store imaginable, run by people from countries around the globe. It was a tiny United Nations, bustling with people, traffic, noise, and blaring music from dawn to dusk, with all kinds of merchandise packing every small store to the ceiling and spilling onto the sidewalks out front. There was an old-fashioned butcher shop next to a store selling wigs (Helen Kang, Janelle's friend from school, and her family, lived above this store) near a store hawking the latest sneakers, discount clothing, tapes, and CDs. Pizza shops and shoe stores dotted Front Street, along with discount variety, five-and-dime, or furniture outlets. Convenience stores and small restaurants, along with an occasional church or school, rounded out the economic hub, and I often walked there in the mornings just to savor the atmosphere. Our little green backyard with porch, glider, swing set, sandbox, and roses seemed far away, but it was literally around the corner and down the block. It was a truly dynamic place in which to raise our very young daughters.

One very special memory I have from living in Kensington is the time I took our daughter, Rhonda, out for a bite to eat at a local restaurant. She was two years old. I had just heard a pastor say that one important key to being a good father was to take each child out for some "time alone with Dad" regularly. (He called them "Dates With Dad.") He said those regular times were key to developing strong bonds with each child, and he recommended starting the practice at age two. That seemed like some easy, practical advice, although age two seemed a bit young. Since Rhonda was two at the time, I decided to give it a try.

I planned a time to take Rhonda around the corner for breakfast and see what happened. (I'm not sure what I told Janelle, who was four, as I'm sure she wanted to come along.) We walked up to Kensington Avenue and under the El tracks, and we found a little storefront restaurant with booths. We settled into a booth and ordered our donuts. Rhonda was small enough that she needed a booster seat as she sat across the table from me. Soon she was reaching up, almost crawling onto the table, trying to push the jukebox buttons at our booth to see them light up. As the milk and donut crumbs ran down her arms and into her bib, I thought to myself, "See, she's too young to know what's going on. She just thinks of this as a game at a toy store or playground." Just as I felt justified in my hasty conclusion, Rhonda looked over at me and uttered words I will remember to my grave, "Daddy, I love you!" Even now, as I write those words, they bring tears to my eyes. That was one holy moment that changed my life forever.

I made sure that our daughters knew that I loved each of them unconditionally and cared about every aspect of their lives. Of course, my relationship with their mother was even more important, so I made sure to take Naomi out regularly, not just on anniversaries or birthdays. Building strong marriages and families takes time and sustained effort at every stage of life. Modeling wholesome Christian family life is a ministry in itself, something sorely needed everywhere, not only in the city. People might listen to our sermons, but they watch how we live.

One more note on keeping a datebook in one's pocket: it's a most valuable ministry tool in the spiritual discipline of time management. The inner city is full of pressing needs and crises, demanding the pastor's attention day and night. To stay sane and spiritually whole, one needs to guard one's stewardship of time with constant diligence. If I was invited to "a very important meeting" or urgently needed at an event, I would find that a quick glance at my datebook and a simple "Sorry, I have a commitment" would excuse me without argument. If I tried instead to explain that I had promised to take my wife to dinner that night, a typical response would be, "Oh, you can do that anytime, but this meeting is more important." Sorry, I have a commitment!

Our youngest daughter, Gwen, was born while we lived in Kensington. She likes to remind us that she's the only one in our family who is

"Philly born and raised"! The rest of us are all "imports," I guess. But our three daughters were all born in urban contexts: Janelle in Columbus, Ohio, and Rhonda in Harrisonburg, VA. While Naomi and I grew up on farms, our daughters never got to experience farm life. This raises the question Naomi and I have been asked countless times: "Can you raise a Christian family in the city?" I will address that question in the next chapter, as it is a very important one to ponder in our rapidly urbanizing world.

Before leaving Kensington, let me note that each of our daughters was born into and surrounded by loving, nurturing communities as they grew. The old African proverb captures a profound truth: "It takes a village to raise a child." Never try raising your children alone! Conversely, never let your environment raise your children for you! Our families and God's family need each other to grow into healthy adults. The American adage that you can "pull yourself up by your own bootstraps" is a dangerous myth. Many people don't even have boots.

When Gwen was born, we had the decided advantage of having Naomi's brother, "Uncle Titus," living with us while attending Messiah College/Temple Campus, by special arrangement. So he was a great help as we adjusted to having a third child in the house. He was much more than a built-in babysitter; he interacted with our girls daily in important ways, playing with them, and entertaining their endless questions. Fun fact about Gwen's birth: Gwen was born at Northeastern Hospital at the corner of Allegheny Avenue and Tulip Street. Unbeknownst to her, seventeen days later, a sweet little baby boy, named Hector Espinosa, was born at that same hospital. Twenty-four years later, Gwen and Hector were joined in holy matrimony. The ironies of history! Many games and jokes made our young family a mostly happy place. The photo below shows the girls pouring and spraying water on Titus on a hot day in our little backyard. It's clear that he enjoyed it as much as they did. Naomi's journal also records that Gwen was a happy baby, easily allowing various people to hold her after church on Sundays. As a toddler, she continued to wiggle her way into everyone's hearts with her smiles and all her friendly chatter. Our church had lots of other children, so our girls made friends at church, at school, and on our block. Our three daughters have been such a blessing to us in our 50+ years in the city, bringing oceans of joy to us and their multitude of friends. "It takes a village" might be easier to find in the city, made up of many smaller "villages" or neighborhoods.

CHAPTER 11

Raising Your Family in the City

C ities are exciting places to live. Cultural, educational, recreational, and vocational resources abound. Cities exhibit the best and worst of human achievement. The oldest and newest exist side by side. Innovation and tradition jostle for position, making for dynamic interplay and activity at every level. Bright lights and music dazzle and amaze. Creativity bubbles up. People love to visit cities; some even want to live there.

Fifty years ago, as we were planning to move to Philadelphia, we got many surprising comments from friends, such as: "God would have to do a miracle in me before I could move there!" "Isn't it a dangerous place to raise children? The city will eat your family alive!" "What a waste of a seminary education!" "What if your daughters wanted to marry one of *them?*" We were saddened by the deep fear hidden behind all of these comments, a fear of the city full of people whom God loves dearly.

"Can you raise a Christian family in the city?" is a question Naomi and I have been asked countless times in our fifty-plus years here in Philadelphia. The answer is obvious: yes, millions of people do it every day. Today, over half the world's population is urban. Even remote villages and farms are becoming "urbanized" via global and social media.

The question also comes loaded with assumptions and presuppositions. A speaker at a missions conference once quipped, "God made the country, man made the suburb, but the devil made the city." Presuppositions such as this one hide behind the question. A deep anti-urban bias has been pervasive in our society, bolstered by Norman Rockwell paintings, folklore, and much of the literature, not to mention the evening news.

People with privilege can easily ask this question, assuming that everyone has options when choosing where to live. But many in our global village cannot freely choose. There is also the common misperception that children need an open space with trees, grass, a dog, and a picket fence to grow up happy. Never mind the fact that no children in the Bible grew up in such an ideal "suburban paradise."

The first sin recorded in the Bible happened in an idyllic garden. The first murder happened on a farm. The first city (Gen. 4) was built for the murderer's protection. The other mention of a farm in the Bible was in Jesus's parable of the man who could not attend the banquet because he "had bought a field," a distraction from the kingdom which Jesus was introducing. Farms can be dangerous; you might want to think twice about raising your family there! By contrast, well over half of the 1,400+ times cities are mentioned in the Bible, they are portrayed positively, as in the seven cities of refuge. "Jerusalem" means "city of peace," and the Psalms portray it as God's favorite city. Even the wicked city of Nineveh is portrayed as undergoing the most profound repentance and revival ever recorded. Even the animals "repented," because God cared deeply for their people and their animals, in stark contrast to God's chosen evangelist, who was not pleased. Perhaps Jonah had the deepest anti-urban bias ever.

In both the Old and New Testaments, we find God deeply concerned for the welfare of the people living in cities, even in cities where only "a few righteous persons" might be found. Jeremiah told the Israelite captives in wicked Babylon to "pray and work hard for the *shalom* of its people; for in the shalom of the city the Israelites would find their own shalom. (Jer. 29:7) In the New Testament, Jesus and the apostles went from town to town and city to city to bring them the gospel and plant urban churches, where the good news could spread.

In Acts, the apostles were accused of "turning cities upside down" and upsetting local economies. Paul's ultimate goal was to take the gospel to Rome, the power center of the empire. We do not find any mention of rural or suburban churches in the New Testament. They are all in cities. And God is building for us the Ultimate City, the New Jerusalem, where I hope we can all live as neighbors someday! As Ray Bakke likes to say, "The Bible began in a garden, but it ends up in a city. You have an urban future, whether you like it or not." So he suggests we should all practice for our heavenly "city-zenship" in our cities here on earth.

The better question, then, is not *whether* to raise a Christian family in the city, but *how*.

A good place to start is by asking the Christian families who already live there how they do it. Learn from the experts on the ground. We watched the families on our street and in our church. We attended urban ministry seminars and read books by experienced practitioners. We wanted our family to be part of God's family as we settled down in the city. ("He led them...to a city where they could settle." Psalm 107:7) We found many families to learn from.

In the urban studies courses I taught at Messiah College/Temple Campus, this question came up frequently, so I developed a teaching outline to help our students (most of whom were White suburbanites) and their parents! to adjust to our cozy campus on North Broad Street. I will share a few points and experiences here for reflection.

One father pulled up on the sidewalk in front of our campus, rolled his window down three inches, and said, "Give me one good reason why I should let my daughter get out of the car *here!*" I replied, "Come join us for lunch, and I will give you more than one!" Over lunch, he was re-assured that some of us lived on campus with our families, had a safe Christian community, and a well-designed program that would be a good place for his daughter to study for at least one semester. So she stayed. (Until the next day, when her boyfriend convinced her to return to Messiah's main campus in Grantham, PA, where she could watch the cows graze on the edge of campus.)

I often gave my students a quiz to get a lively discussion going. Here are a few sample questions:

<u>What makes a Christian family?</u> (See Ephesians 5 and 6)

John Drescher, in his book, *Seven Things Children Need*, says they need significance, security, acceptance, love, praise, discipline, and God. Bob DeMoss says the top priorities for Christian parents are: Praying for their children daily, Loving them unconditionally, and Modelling Christian behavior. Which of the above are easier in (1) the country? (2) the city? (3) the suburbs? (4) on an island? Why?

<u>Which theory helps develop stronger Christian children?</u>

Theory X: Shield them from the evils of the world and fill their minds with Christian teaching.

Theory Y: Expose them to the real world but guide them in their development.

Those opening questions always sparked a vigorous conversation, since many of my students came to the Philadelphia Campus precisely to get out of the "Grantham Bubble" of our main campus, as they often called it. They were eager to experience Temple University and our great city, while still being Messiah College students in our secure community, the best of three worlds in one. (More about this in a coming chapter.)

I would then continue to explain some of the key principles that Naomi and I tried to live by as our three daughters attended local public schools and regularly attended our church and youth group. Our neighborhood was mostly African American, but the church, school, and Temple were all multicultural. So our daughters grew up as "third-culture kids," kids who grow up in a culture different from the dominant culture of their origins. This brings challenges and blessings. 3C kids often feel like they belong nowhere and everywhere at the same time. What is their "true identity"? But it can help prepare them for life in today's world.

We tried to instill and model what it means to be a family in ministry together, rather than pitting the ministry against the family, to interact with all our neighbors openly, learn from and grow with them, rather than preach to them. We would invite them to church, youth group, or day camp, echoing a motto of the Mennonite Church at the time: "Our Family can be Your Family!" Loving God and neighbor became both a daily opportunity and a daily challenge. Our faith and our daughters' faith grew in the daily experience. We faced difficult challenges alongside our daughters, having open discussions with them about things such as racism, alcoholism, drugs, and street violence. Naomi would say to our girls as they went out the door for public school, "Remember who you are!" and pray with them, not knowing what the day might hold. Were we naive to use this approach with our girls?

One day, Janelle came home from school with a story. "Today, there was a fight in the hall. My friends called me over to intervene, as they knew I would not take sides, but neither would I avoid the conflict." Maybe we weren't being naive. Sometimes we would need to go to the school with our daughter to talk to a teacher or find creative ways to address issues as they arose. Even though the outside of a public school may look forbidding, inside, we always found kind and caring teachers and administrators who faced the many challenges of inner-city schools with grace and courage. They are urban heroes. We were learning and growing together as a family. Parenting is sometimes challenging, but nothing is more rewarding and fulfilling. Unconditional love goes a long way and pays huge dividends lasting a lifetime.

Raising children is a daunting task, no matter your context, and it requires much wisdom, grace, and love. Each child is different, as is every set of parents. Personalities and dispositions vary. No one can be perfectly prepared for the challenges and joys of parenting. No wonder it takes a village and a lot of prayer to raise well-balanced, mature young people in today's world. Also, no two cities are the same. No one-size-fits-all recipe can guarantee a happy family. Cities contain the best and worst of human behavior, full of wonderful attractions and resources along with the noise, pollution, crime, and grime that any concentration of humans will entail. Children who grow up in cities are constantly surrounded by possibilities and pitfalls, needing all the wise guidance and counsel available at home, at school, at church, and in the street. There is little opportunity for boredom in the hustle and bustle of daily life and much opportunity for growth.

It turns out that the most important environment for your young children is inside the four walls of your home, not the four miles surrounding your house. That is true wherever you may live, from the cabin in the woods to the condominium on top of the newest tower downtown. Dedicated, loving parents, spending quality time together, one-on-one time with each child, as well as regular dinner and family nights together, are a strong foundation on which to build. "The family that prays together stays together" is more than just a bumper sticker. Children need structure, predictable patterns, and loving but firm guidance from mature adults. The Bible says we are to "bring them up in the fear and admonition of the Lord." It takes a church and a village.

After graduating from public schools, each daughter took their freshman year at Temple, right across the street, where they got reduced tuition because of my connections with Messiah College. After that, each attended a Christian college for their sophomore year to experience at least one year of Christian education. Two attended Eastern Mennonite University, and one went to Messiah University. I remember with a chuckle the day we got a phone call from Janelle during her first week at EMU. She said, "Dad, I want to take a walk, but there is no place to walk." I was stunned because she had wide-open spaces and a grassy hill behind her dorm. But she felt exposed and alone. She wanted to walk surrounded by people, just like back home in Philly!

That was hilariously ironic! That very day, a new student at Messiah/Temple had told me the exact same thing. "I want to take a walk, but there is no place to walk!" I explained that I took walks all the time, all over Temple and around the neighborhood, and also around Temple's track, which was just around the corner and a block away. Our daughter and that student perfectly illustrated what is so often the case: urban and rural people holding opposing fears and misconceptions about each other. They might venture into each other's "territory," but hurry home before dark.

Rhonda attended Messiah College and would sometimes tell me, "Dad, can you take me back to Philly, please? I'm so tired of explaining to my professors or my friends that they have totally skewed perceptions of city life. They make the city look terrible!" Ironic and sad. Rhonda ended up taking a few semesters "back home" at the Philly Campus.

After college, each daughter began testing adult life in the city: looking for a job, mingling with friends, testing friendships and boyfriends, visiting churches, and engaging in short-term mission assignments, trusting God to help them find their niche. It was exciting (and sometimes exhausting) to walk with them through these testing periods. We tried to be supportive at each stage in their journeys. Whenever a potential new "boyfriend" appeared, we would ask our daughter to bring him around for visits, invite him to church, have him join us at a picnic, and so on. We wanted to get to know each young man personally as the relationships grew.

Our daughters wondered if we were really okay with inter-racial dating. We said if the young man was a sincere Christian with a solid moral character (and maybe already part of our church), how could we say no on the basis of race? Wouldn't it be hypocritical to say he could be part of God's family and our church family, but not our biological family? And so a new chapter of family life in the city began. (Side note: early in our Philadelphia years, some seasoned Black members of our church predicted that when our daughters reached dating age, we would move out of the city, because that's what Mennonites did. They called these Mennonites "Gypsies.")

Godly homes and godly churches can help stabilize the ever-changing urban landscape. Churches are still seen as social and spiritual anchors, even as populations shift over time. Multicultural urban churches, modeled after the church at Antioch in Acts 13*, can be important vehicles for the twenty-first-century church to carry out the Great Commission Jesus gave us in Matthew 28. Now, as back then, the good news of the kingdom can still "turn cities upside down," transforming a broken world into health and wholeness. Dividing walls will come down, enemies turn into friends, hoarding change to sharing; peace may even break out instead of endless war! Loving God and neighbor are still the most important mandates for peace on earth, especially in our urban world.

Eventually, after navigating many relational waters with our young-adult daughters, we gained three wonderful sons-in-law and nine amazing grandchildren, I couldn't imagine life without them. Here is what our growing family looked like on our vacation, summer of 2019:

*Antioch of Syria (Acts 11 and 13) was the third-largest city of the Roman Empire with more than 500,000 residents, racially diverse and a pluralistic bustling trade center. It was divided by walls into four quadrants–Greek, Syrian, African, and Jewish. The church in Antioch became a main headquarters for the New Testament church. They saw ethnic division as a barrier to overcome, as shown by their multi-ethnic leadership team (Acts 13:1) drawn from the various quadrants, as the barriers came down in Christ. This is the church where they were first called Christians, and where the first missionary/church-planting team was sent out to carry the gospel to other cities. (Summary adapted from *The Word in Life Study Bible* notes on Acts 13. Thomas Nelson, 1994.)

CHAPTER 12

Pastor on Diamond Street

When we arrived, Diamond Street Mennonite Church, while located in a predominantly Black neighborhood, was racially mixed, with a history of strong leaders, both Black and White. Raymond Jackson, the first Black lead pastor and a "favorite son" raised up from within the congregation, had led the church into vigorous engagement with the civil rights movement during the turbulent 60's when riots erupted in the neighborhood. There was some blending of cultural traditions, but the singing and worship styles were largely imported from Lancaster County. While some younger Black members had gone off to Mennonite schools and colleges or into Mennonite Voluntary Service, the "flavor" instilled by the early sister workers and visiting rural pastors had left a lasting legacy. Emma Rudy and Alma Ruth, the two women who labored seven days a week to reach children and youth — in reality, they were the actual church planters — are still revered to this day by those who remember them. They were both devout, sincere Mennonite women whose plain dress and head coverings created much curiosity. Sometimes people came to the church to see what motivated these White women to live and work in a Black community. These faithful "sister workers" touched many lives with the love of Jesus. Some of those local children and youth stayed and became leaders in the church; others moved on and became leaders elsewhere.

My Amish heritage had hardly prepared me to fit into this context. However, our years at Burnside Mennonite Church in Columbus, our three-year sojourn in Nigeria, and my teaching at East High School in Columbus (95% Black), along with other cross-cultural experiences, did offer some helpful orientation. But there was still much to learn about the realities of our new community of work and worship. Fortunately, there were long-time "seasoned saints" at the Diamond Street church–Black, White, and others–to facilitate our adjustment, giving friendly advice, and helping us to fit into the various ministries already well established. Soon, we felt right at home in our new church family. We were among friends and "fellow laborers" in God's urban vineyard. Our corner church had a big sign out front that said simply, "Come to Jesus." We were known as the "Come to Jesus Church," not a bad nickname to have.

My first big plunge came with the summer day camp, which Diamond Street Mennonite Church (DSMC) ran every year in July and August. Eight weeks of high-energy kids, ages six to sixteen, filling our three-story row-house church five days a week during the hottest months in the inner city proved to be a wonderful, though stressful, introduction to the rigors of urban ministry. By the end of the summer, our staff was totally exhausted, desperately needing a week off to recover.

The church leaders thought that a good way for me to get to know DSMC's culture would be to join Daniel Grimes, home from college for the summer, in running the summer day camp. They were so right! I got to know the church families and the families in the neighborhood who sent their children to the camp. Also tossed into the mix was a new VSer (Mennonite Voluntary Service worker) Jay Burkholder. Jay and I were two new White staff members joining seasoned African American staff who had grown up and served for years in the church. You can easily guess who learned the most that first summer. Daniel Grimes and Opher Hinton (Daniel's assistant) were two experienced young adults who had been through the summer day camp as campers and later as camp counselors, so they knew how things were to be done. They knew what would work and what wouldn't, whom to call on for specific needs, and in general what a vast network of kind-hearted souls it took to minister effectively to 80 high-energy kids during the hottest weeks of summer.

After that sudden plunge into summertime ministry in the big city, it was time to focus on becoming a full-time inner-city pastor. I set up an office on the second floor of our little row-home-turned-storefront church in a small room with a bay window so I could keep an eye on the front door and the foot traffic outside our building. This gave me a bit of privacy for study, sermon preparation, typing bulletins and letters, phone calls, and other office tasks. Since our little blue-walled sanctuary was on the first floor, my office needed to be on the second, even though that meant a long flight of stairs. This arrangement worked fairly well, except on days when I had to run up and down the stairs to answer the doorbell.

I was standing on the shoulders of giants. The church had a long and storied history. It began in 1935 in response to African American children and young people attending church or church programs at the Norris Square Mennonite Mission (mostly White). In 1942, it was relocated to 1814 W. Diamond Street in the heart of a Black, inner-city neighborhood. The sign which Luke Stoltzfus (former pastor, now bishop) found in the church basement when their family moved into the city in the 1950's said something like, "Mennonite Mission for Coloreds." So, it is clear that the church was started from White segregationist impulses, but when we arrived in 1975, there was a good ethnic mix with many of the leaders being from local African American families who had been in the church from its earliest days on Diamond Street. Recent pastors had included Black and White men, some of whom had lived in the neighborhood and had raised their families there.

Raymond Jackson was the first black person raised up from within the church to serve as senior pastor, but he had left one year before we came to serve as lead pastor, ironically, in the church we had attended in Columbus, Ohio: Burnside Mennonite. (I say this was ironic because, in a sense, we had "traded churches" but had never met each other.) His assistant pastor, Charles Baynard, was still serving at the church here and was my assistant pastor for many years, later to become the lead pastor himself. Charles was also African American, but had been raised among Amish Mennonite farmers in the Lancaster area, and thus was not from Philadelphia but had married Barbara Allen, who was a Diamond Street original. The church was no longer an ethnic-specific church when we came in 1975. We worked on interracial and multicultural issues during our years at Diamond Street. We learned much about the deep racial issues embedded in our society from slavery days until now, and the vigorous, sustained intentionality required to begin dismantling the evils of American racism, even in the church.

Our corner storefront church was a blip on the radar screen in the big city. There were many large church buildings and cathedrals scattered throughout the urban landscape, as well as storefronts like ours, in various sizes in between. Recent research shows there are around 3,000 houses of worship in the city, most of them Christian. One large famous cathedral was the Episcopal Church of the Advocate, immediately across the street from our corner church. I asked our church members what they knew about the other church and discovered there was little interaction between the two churches.

I went over to meet Father Paul M. Washington, the famous African American priest who presided there for many years. He was surprised and delighted to meet me, and we became friends, eventually joining forces to host an annual street festival together. The Church of the Advocate used to have standing-room-only crowds when it opened in 1897. But when we came, more than a century later, they had a very small group gathering on Sundays in the parish house next door to the church for the liturgy and communion. The huge cathedral was used mainly for public events. Father Washington was an icon of resistance in the black community, but that did not translate into large crowds for worship on most Sundays. His story is wonderfully told in *Other Sheep I Have* (Washington and Gracie, Temple University Press, 1994). He is also memorialized in a large, colorful mural at the intersection of Ridge and Cumberland Streets in the Strawberry Mansion section of North Philadelphia.

To expand our ministry, we began attending urban ministry conferences and various Lancaster Conference events, invited John Perkins of Mississippi (founder of Voice of Calvary Ministries) to visit and preach, and visited other urban Mennonite churches in New York and other cities. We raised money to buy a church van, a yellow school bus, and an old jalopy utility van. Keeping the vehicles serviced and running was a challenge. I remember lying under that bus on the street in front of the church with Charles Baynard, William Jackson (both mechanics), and others at night, getting the bus ready for day camp trips. The Friday field trips and longer camping trips all made for fun, frustration, and lots of great memories. Staff and students formed lifelong relationships that transformed many of us over the months.

As I visited other churches around the city and got to know other pastors, I learned that our small church had touched countless lives since it acquired the corner rowhouse at 1814 W. Diamond in 1942, the year I was born. Quite a few pastors and other leaders (not Mennonite) told me that they got their start at DSMC. They remembered the names of Alma Ruth and Emma Rudy, as well as many of the Bible school songs and memory verses they learned there. The gospel salt, light, and yeast had spread far and wide. I was standing on holy ground, cultivated by earnest urban ministry pioneers. Their labor was bearing fruit.

Sunday mornings were a joyful challenge. The singing at our church had been mostly acapella hymns and choruses learned in summer Bible school or camp. There was no accompaniment unless someone was present who could open the piano and play for us. We found out that while singing was an important part of worship, many were eager for some Black gospel and more contemporary songs. So when Tom Fitch (White Temple grad student) blew in during a snowstorm one morning and began playing a Black gospel song during the offering, the church exploded into newness and exuberant rejoicing. It is safe to say that our church was never the same after that. Tom ended up directing our fledgling choir and building it into a multi-ethnic gospel powerhouse, releasing new energy into our worship and witness. The choir went on tours, recorded several tapes, and even sang at the Mennonite World Conference in France in 1984. Contextualizing the gospel is key to reaching people's hearts, and music often plays a central part. There is nothing like hearing the Good News in your mother tongue and in the music of your people. Tom had learned to play all types of music, so he could blend the various cultures represented at Diamond Street into a rich mix of genres, especially highlighting Black gospel. Below is a photo from the cover of a cassette tape recorded by the choir. Tom is the first person in the front row left.

ALL GOD'S CHILDREN
The Diamond Street Mennonite Church Choir
Tom Fitch, Director
SIDE ONE
READING FROM PSALM 61:1-2
I'VE GOT CONFIDENCE
William Jackson, Soloist
MY HOPE IS BUILT*
IT'S GONNA RAIN
Walter Baynard, Soloist
JOY, JOY
Beatrice Macon, Soloist
SIDE TWO
READING FROM JOHN 14:1-3
HE WATCHETH OVER ME*
Marie Clemens, Soloist
DEEP RIVER
Marie Clemens, Soloist
THE LOVE MEDLEY
Art Griffin, Soloist
ALL GOD'S CHILDREN
Beatrice Macon, Soloist
*Directed by Wanda Bryant

Music is something I have been interested in all my life, ever since Esther Hilty came to teach at Plainview School back home. When she taught us to sight-read (shaped notes), and we sang through the hymnal, a whole new world opened up to me. She even visited Amish church services, and we had "contests" with her about whether all seven tones of the diatonic scale were in the old Amish German church chants. So, instead of the slow Gregorian chants we sang in church, suddenly a whole new world of harmonious hymnody opened up. Later, I was exposed to classical, jazz, soul, black gospel, rock, hip-hop, reggae, and other genres. As I learned about the origins and contexts of these works, I adjusted my tastes to enjoy them to varying degrees, just as I came to enjoy the many genres of literature. I became increasingly amazed by the variety of creativity across human cultures, realizing that this is yet another illustration that we are all made in the creative image of our Creator. I am grateful for the doors God opened for me into other cultures over the years, for it helped me be more receptive to the varieties of music I was to encounter not only at Diamond Street, but eventually among the many other ethnic and multicultural churches, which I would get to know and love

It was a new experience to be the lead pastor of a church like Diamond Street. No seminary can fully train you for the peculiarities of any given church, especially if the seminaries are run by White, mostly rural denominations, and your church is a multicultural church deep in the heart of a Black inner city community. I believe that "on-the-job training" is required to fully fit into any specific church. After living in Kensington for the first five years, we moved to 2027 N. Carlisle Street in 1980, where we renovated a three-story row house in the middle of the block, with the help of Reynold Zimmerman, a VSer, along with members of our church and visits from my family in Ohio, a kind of "inner-city barn-raising."

We now lived on the edge of Temple University, just three blocks from the church. Finally, we could practice "incarnational ministry" by moving into the neighborhood where the church was located. Our block was mostly African-American, with a few other ethnicities sprinkled in. Some families from our church lived on the block. We got to know our neighbors, who worked together to improve the block and the neighborhood. I could walk to and from the church for my work. When we divided the church into small groups for weekly Bible study, one group met on our block. Here's a snapshot of a cookout on our front stoop on Carlisle Street.

The 2000 block of N. Carlisle Street was an amazing block. Our daughters loved playing with other children on the block, jumping double-dutch, playing in the open fire-hydrant spray during hot weather, hopscotch, dodgeball, and other creative games, often improvised on the spot. Sometimes our girls thought we were too strict as parents by making them come in at bedtime on school nights; they wanted to stay out late and play. Block parties in the summer drew all the neighbors together to share food, stories, and develop friendships. Many of our family's lifelong friendships were formed on that precious block. Don't get me wrong; it was not a perfect block. There were also disputes, arguments, and fights from time to time, as is common among humans. But the block stuck together and looked out for each other's kids and cars, as neighbors should. Borrowing eggs, sugar, or butter were common. Neighbors really cared.

Preparing sermons, Bible studies, and prayer meetings make up only a small part of what is expected of an inner-city pastor. Every day, there are doorbells and phone calls, walk-ins and walk-outs, crises to intervene in, plumbing and heating emergencies, along with the despair of poverty and hopelessness pervading neglected inner cities. The pastor is expected to be on call 24/7, to never get sick, to be a wellspring of wisdom and encouragement, to know all the answers from the Bible, raise a perfect family, have time to visit those who were sick or in prison, have endless patience and love for everyone, plus be able to spend quality time with God and loved ones. No wonder pastors burn out, especially those who have small churches with limited staff and resources in a sea of endless demands. Balancing work and home life becomes a matter of daily discipleship and stewardship, a holy dance.

Walking in the neighborhood around the church was a very important part of being "present" in the city. Living within walking distance of the church brought both blessings and challenges. North Philly residents often sit on their front steps, chatting with neighbors, especially when the weather warms up. Whenever I walked to the church, I would greet those I met and sometimes stop to visit briefly. I learned a lot about my neighbors and neighborhood that I could not have learned from driving by in a car. Some people were surprised that a pastor would walk the streets or stop for a chat. Sometimes I needed to drive the four blocks to our church in order to get to a meeting on time; otherwise, I'd have to stop and talk with too many neighbors if I walked. That was a good problem to have, but still required boundaries and balance.

Another problem with living in the neighborhood was that whenever there was a crisis, I was usually available. Since I lived nearby, people could find me day or night, and they did! A phone call in the middle of the night usually meant a sudden death, accident, illness, or other calamity requiring my urgent attention. Finding time for self, God, family, and even sleep was sometimes a challenge. Even trying to escape by blending anonymously into the downtown crowd on my day off did not always work. I would bump into neighbors or church members on the sidewalk or in a department store elevator! So much for being "just a number" in the city.

The daily routine was hardly ever routine. I announced and scheduled regular "office hours" for people to come see me, but emergencies often intervened, thus necessitating flexibility at all times. I might get to the office at 9:00 a.m. and begin working on the sermon for the upcoming Sunday, only to get a phone call or a ring on the doorbell, or to discover a malfunction of the heating, water, or electrical systems. In the early days, I did not have an office secretary and had to handle all issues myself.

Since I was the primary leader of the church (Charles Baynard, my associate pastor, had a full-time job in addition to ministry), it meant that it fell to me to see that sermons, Bible studies, Sunday school materials, the weekly bulletin, church cleaning and maintenance, record-keeping, and reporting were all kept on track. Fortunately, I had taught myself to type, using a photo of a typewriter keyboard from a Sears catalog in my youth back home, so I could type minutes, bulletins, reports, sermon outlines, and other records and did not need someone to transcribe my scribbled notes. But there were also pastoral visits to hospitals, prisons, and elderly sick or shut-ins, not to mention picking up local seniors on Sunday mornings who had no other way to get to church. Fortunately, we had many volunteers, both church members and VSers (persons serving with Mennonite Voluntary Service programs, and living in VS houses in the city), to help with many of these tasks, or I would likely have burned out the first year.

Three very simple ideas spurred our small corner church into engagement and growth in the late 70's: (1) Reorganizing for growth, (2) Surveying the community, and (3) Opening a community center. I will offer a brief summary of each to show how a "mustard seed" idea can grow into a "mighty tree," borrowing a metaphor from Jesus.

<u>Getting Organized.</u> "If you want a blessing, get organized!" This opening line from Bishop Leslie Francisco III, our visiting speaker from Hampton, VA, at our district pastors' retreat, drew a few chuckles. But he was serious. He went on to explain how he used to pray for God to bring new people to their small church. God gave him a jolting revelation one day. It went something like this: "You can't even get your sock drawer or your closet in order, let alone My House! How can I bring new people to your church when you're not organized to receive them?" Wow. Bishop Leslie told us how their church reorganized, training greeters, ushers, nursery workers, Sunday School teachers, parking attendants, and others, all with the expectation of welcoming newcomers and growing them in their faith. The results were dramatic. Today, that church is the largest Mennonite church on the East Coast. Prayer is powerful. Putting legs under your prayers is part of the answer. His words echo those of Herb Miller, who used to run seminars on church growth under the banner, "Getting Ready for Company." Just as you get your house and family ready for company, so you should get your church ready for those God wanted to "add to their number," as was the norm in the early church. (See Acts 2:47) At Diamond Street, we completely redrew our church organizational chart from hierarchy to a perforated circle, with interconnected ministry teams, which released many gifts formerly dormant in our church. New vision and new growth emerged as we prayerfully joined hands and watched the Spirit move.

<u>Community Survey.</u> At an urban ministry conference, John Perkins challenged us by saying, "You don't need to hire trained consultants to make your church a dynamic part of your community. Simply form a small research team to pray, then go out two by two, from door to door, asking three simple questions: What is the biggest need in this neighborhood? How could the churches help meet that need? How can we pray for you?" So we printed up small questionnaires identifying us as a church, got our clipboards, and headed out. We asked our neighbors to help us with a simple community survey. The results were astounding. The overwhelming consensus was that the key need along Diamond

Street was housing. We were not even thinking of housing. What could our small group do about urban housing? As we prayed about how to respond, a local politician called to ask whether they could use our church for a community meeting on housing. We said sure! And they did. Which eventually led to the next idea.

<u>Community Center.</u> The neighbors wanted us to help save the abandoned buildings in the 1600 block of Diamond Street (the next block over) from planned demolition, which would waste taxpayer dollars and produce nothing good for the neighborhood. Their biggest concern was the large four-story historic former Masonic hall on the corner, along with the vacant houses next to it. Talk about a giant challenge! We formed a small community housing committee, made up of church members and neighbors, to think, pray, and act. As we met to plan, one of our neighbors made a bold suggestion. She said, "The Bible says, 'Ye have not because ye ask not.' Why don't we just ask the City Council to give us that big building, so we can turn it into a Community Services Center?" Silence. You could hear a pin drop. Slowly, the brazen idea began to germinate, and that is exactly what we did. We arranged a meeting with members of the City Council and explained our idea to them. Now it was the Council's turn to be dumbfounded. They huddled for a quick conference, then gave their reply. They gave us a few weeks to see how much money we could raise, to show we were serious. Then they gave us the building under the city's Gift Property Program, for the cost of transferring the deed! Absolutely astonishing! And frightening! Our knees were trembling. Below is a photo of me, signing the agreement.

We spent the next few years raising money, forming boards and committees, and renovating the former Masonic hall into a building to house the church and serve the community with social services. We eventually ran a holistic health center, various youth programs, activities such as pottery-making for senior citizens, a gymnasium for youth on the top floor, and others. We also opened a Habitat for Humanity office in the building after helping launch a North Philadelphia branch, which eventually built new houses in our neighborhood. All of this from a simple survey question: What are the needs of this community, and how can churches help?

We were able to practice in new ways our growing conviction that churches should engage their surrounding neighborhoods with loving, living concern for their souls, and also for their bodies, their minds, their families. Loving God and neighbor means caring about the physical, spiritual, mental, and social needs of every neighbor. A holistic view of ministry was taking root.

The dozen years I spent as lead pastor at DSMC were among the richest and hardest of my life. I would not trade them for anything in the world. They are priceless. I could never find enough words to fully describe the thousands of answered prayers, daily miracles, and endless growing pains as our storefront congregation grew in size and influence, eventually filling that community center with services that touched lives seven days a week, all year round. It was exhausting and exhilarating. Also humbling. We realized we were part of something much bigger than our small church. God was on the move. One of our favorite worship songs became "Move With The Cloud," a reference to God's Spirit leading the Israelites out of bondage in Egypt into the promised land of Canaan. I am not going to explain in detail the community resistance that arose from time to time, nor the laughable rumors that began to spread. One of our church members heard a rumor circulating at City Hall: "Those Mennonites are planning to take over all of North Philadelphia from river to river!" We felt, on most days, that we were just barely hanging on, wondering where our next grant would come from or how we could staff the many emerging programs. Since Mennonites were a small, relatively unknown denomination to many, we had to build trust by explaining our faith history and assuring our neighbors that we were not a cult or secret society.

I could never fully capture in writing my years as pastor of Diamond Street Mennonite Church. No two days were the same. I will note a few samples here to give a glimpse into my busy life, mostly from our days at the corner storefront, before we moved into the large community center building. One day, I was alone at the old church when I heard footsteps up on the third floor. My office was on the second floor, and I was sure I was the only one in the building, but the footsteps above indicated otherwise. I felt a brief flash of panic, but I prayed, and instantly the panic left. I quickly called Margaret Allen, director of Bethany Child Care Center, a few blocks away, and told her to stay on the phone while I checked who the intruders might be. (This was before cell phones, so I left the receiver off the hook so she could hear me in the background.) I yelled up the stairs, "Who's there?" and several teenage boys answered. I asked what they were doing up there, and they said they were looking for "Alex" (or some name I didn't recognize as belonging to anyone I knew at the church). They said they often came here to play pool with him, but I said there was no one here by that name and asked how they got in. It turns out they came in through a skylight on the flat roof of our three-story corner rowhouse church. They helped me close up some windows they had opened, and followed me downstairs as I invited them to come back next Sunday for church and Sunday school. They said sure, but when I opened the front door for them to leave, they ran away like frightened deer. I realized that the fear had left me and entered into them as the Holy Spirit took over in that startling interruption.

One day I walked around in our neighborhood to meet people and invite them to church. There was a small bar on a side street near the church, and on a whim, I decided I think Jesus would go in there as well. I entered, went around the tables, and handed out leaflets, making small talk with folks and inviting them to read them and come talk to me if they wanted to know more. One person said, "Aren't you from that church down the street?" I said yes, and they asked what I was doing in the bar. I said, "Bringing you Good News!" They replied, "This is the first time anyone ever gave me good news in a bar!" There was good humor, and I'm not sure I ever saw them again (nor the two guys mentioned in the last paragraph, for that matter). But many people on the street were very glad to see me, sometimes inviting me into their homes to pray for a loved one or for a special need. I never entered a home in North Philadelphia where people did not want me to pray for them. African American culture is so rooted in the church that there seems to be an openness to the things of God that is sometimes missing in other cultures.

I remember one young couple who came breathlessly into the church one day, asking me to marry them. When they sensed my hesitation, they wondered if it was the money? They would give me more! I explained that I only did weddings for people I knew well, with whom I had done a series of counseling sessions, and who were part of a strong Christian church that could help sustain their marriage through the ups and downs. They seemed bewildered, shook their heads, and went on their way, looking for a more cooperative pastor. This incident reminds me of another one, where a young man from the community stopped in and asked what he needed to do to join our church. "Do I need to get baptized again? No problem! I've been baptized many times!" (I guess he was an Ana-Anabaptist!) Clearly, people bring all kinds of preconceptions about churches and pastors.

One day, the phone rang, and an older woman's voice asked whether we were a Mennonite Church, saying she had found us in a directory or had heard about us somewhere. I began to explain that we were indeed a bona fide Mennonite congregation, whereupon she began pumping me with many questions, beginning with "Aren't you in a Black neighborhood? Do you have Black members?" I replied affirmatively, which completely threw her off. She declared that there could not be Black Mennonites because you had to be born a Mennonite to be a true Mennonite. I corrected her by stating that no, you had to be born again to become a member, and that anyone who accepted Christ as Savior and Lord could join the church. She was not convinced and told me to go talk to her nephew, who held a high position at nearby Temple University. She was going to call him and tell him to expect my visit so he could verify whether I was indeed a Mennonite pastor and was telling the truth. This eventually led to a very interesting and meaningful meeting between me and a Vice President at Temple, who had his own sad family history of interactions with Mennonites in NYC. He assured me that his elderly aunt was a very fussy woman and that it was just like her to call me. Please pay her no mind. It turns out he was from one of the famous Niebuhr families in New York, but I cannot elaborate here.

Our many rich and full years at Diamond Street Mennonite Church cannot be adequately captured in words. The bonds that were formed, lives touched and transformed, new and/or renewed people added to our number, relationships built with the neighborhood and neighboring churches–all bear witness to the power of the gospel. When God's redeemed people form a visible and viable presence in any location, the yeast of the gospel begins to "leaven" both the church and the local community. New life flows into and out of the church.

CHAPTER 13

Off Spooky Nook Road with EMM

A surprising turn of events occurred during the summer of 1987. I was asked to consider serving as Director of Home Ministries at Eastern Mennonite Missions (EMM). The invitation came right when I was facing possible burnout as the pastor of Diamond Street Church. There had been enough stress with church and community center issues that I felt depleted and in need of a change. While the church continued to grow and we had many wonderful stories to share, some neighborhood residents were unhappy with the community center project, afraid that "these Mennonites were going to take over all of North Philadelphia from river to river!" Humerous and sad. It is one time when Mennonite stereotypes perhaps hindered our work: people did not know much about Mennonites, so the emergence of a strong new community presence in the heart of a large Black neighborhood caused some misgivings and suspicions. Understandably so. There were community and church members on the board, but when we received a large anonymous gift to repair the elevator, the word "anonymous" stirred mistrust. There was a rumor that, since we were using a side entrance to the building's basement level at first, we might just be a cult. At any rate, I felt very worn down with the stress of both church and community center concerns weighing on me daily.

So when I got a call from EMM about considering an open position with them, it came as a breath of fresh possibility. As I recall, President

Paul G. Landis and his wife, Joanne, wanted to meet with Naomi and me, and said they thought I might be a good fit to direct the Home Ministries (HM) department, as David Shenk was moving on to direct the Overseas Ministries (OM) department. HM was charged with overseeing church planting along the East Coast and promoting missional outreach among the nearly 200 congregations in the Lancaster Mennonite Conference (now LMC). I was approached as a candidate because many EMM church plants were in cities, and perhaps it was time to have someone with more urban experience to direct the work. It all made sense, since it sometimes seemed a bit difficult for LMC and EMM to understand those of us in urban church contexts. But there were a few problems. DSMC did not seem ready to see me step down from the leadership at the church, even though they saw the "good sense" of the idea. The bigger problem was that we were not ready to move our family to EMM headquarters at Salunga, PA, in the heart of Lancaster County. We wanted to remain rooted in Philadelphia, the city to which we felt called.

Needless to say, this sparked a difficult summer of discernment for us and for the church. We prayed, we talked, we discussed possible scenarios. Eventually, most of the church members agreed that it made sense, even if they did not want me to step aside as pastor. Eventually, we floated the idea of my directing the HM department from an office in Philadelphia, with occasional trips to headquarters in Salunga as needed. With the advent of computers, the internet, and email — in addition to phone connections — it began to seem feasible. After much discussion, we agreed on terms and opened an office next to the YES Discipleship Center in Philadelphia. YES was an EMM program patterned after YWAM, sending teams of young adults to serve abroad. Galen Burkholder was the director of YES and lived at the discipleship center. Occasionally, we could travel to Salunga together. Usually, however, I would commute to Salunga by Amtrak one day a week for staff meetings, but I did most of my work and travel from the Philadelphia office. It was yet another new chapter in the story of my life. For the most part, it worked very well. Most of the urban pastors and church planters I worked with were happy to have someone at HM who understood city church life. And I was glad for the opportunity of working alongside other urban ministers in various settings. This led to fruitful dialogue and cross-fertilization of ideas on how to make urban churches more effective at revitalizing our cities.

I began to look forward to the train trips to Salunga, and to many of the East Coast cities where I needed to travel for meetings. I discovered that I could travel by train for less than it would cost to drive. On trips to New England, for example, I could take another EMM person with me if meetings called for it. Two of us could travel by train for less than the mileage charge for using an EMM vehicle. Train travel was less stressful than fighting traffic, looking for parking, and turning in mileage. One could sleep, read, write, or talk on the train and reach one's destination feeling refreshed.

Since we lived a few blocks from a subway station, I could get up early, catch the subway to 30th Street Station, and be on Amtrak before most of the city woke up. I dictated most of my memos, letters, and meeting minutes on the train, and just swapped tapes with the HM secretary every time I went to Salunga. This was a workable arrangement. The biggest adjustment seemed to be at Salunga, where the close-knit staff was used to huddling quickly for a meeting whenever needed and not used to waiting for the regular Tuesday visits when I came to headquarters. So we made it work for more than three years. Those were very good years. I treasure the relationships and memories created in my work with EMM. After leaving HM, I continued to serve on the EMM board for years.

Twelve years earlier, I had been recruited for Diamond Street by both Bishop Luke Stoltzfus and Chester Wenger, who was Director of Home Ministries at the time. For the first few years, EMM partially supported me as a pastor, since Diamond Street was still considered a "mission" as it transitioned to a church. A few years later, EMM began scaling back financial support for urban pastors and bishops (Bishop Luke had been supported throughout his years as bishop in the city), and the church and I had to scramble to make ends meet. All this is simply to say that I "understood" the EMM "ethos," to a degree. But 12 years in the city had urbanized me to the point that I felt some culture shock every time I went to Salunga, even though EMM was a familiar organization. As I was setting up my Salunga office, I asked my HM secretary if it was okay to have a radio in my office. (I like to play soft music as I work. The music also symbolizes ongoing prayers rising.) She said yes, and soon I heard rumors, "Freeman wants a radio in his office!" with apparent happy surprise. The "corporate culture" at EMM was a cluster of offices and cubicles full of diligent, committed, quiet workers, hunched over their desks, often arriving early and leaving late to ensure projects and reports were completed on time. EMM had mission work underway in many countries worldwide, as well as across the US. Fund-raising and coordinating all departments required a large and dedicated staff. It was wonderful to have my call to "missions" expanded through this opportunity to serve with an organization that carries the gospel to the four corners of the globe.

I enjoyed getting to know the HM staff, about eight or ten persons at the time, all with different job descriptions designed to help HM spur LMC regional districts to plant new churches, help new church plants to grow, help older churches to get revitalized through community outreach, and other "missional" efforts in our American churches. Also, we needed to plan regional and conference-wide events related to outreach ministries, church growth, and fundraising. The staff was a committed and happy group of sincere, younger, gifted persons, all eager to help our conference churches be more vibrant and effective. On my days at the Salunga office, we would often gather in one room or office to eat our sack lunches, pray, and exchange stories. We had a lot of fun, laughing and getting to know each other as a team. I remember at least one occasion where someone from another office came and tapped on our door, only to stick their head in and say, with a chuckle, "You are having way too much fun back here!" I think it was meant as a compliment. I enjoyed working with a great team. (See photo below, 1989)

My main task as director was to coordinate all departmental activities, raise funds, and balance the million-dollar-plus budget, and to travel to various outlying regions to support the many new churches LMC/EMM had planted from Maine to Mississippi. It was a challenging time as our department recruited, trained, deployed, and supported many candidates who felt called to plant a new church. Finding the right people for specific locations was both exhilarating and daunting. Every summer we ran a one-week retreat for all church planters, known as "School For Apostles." There, we got to know each other, shared stories, offered training, and ministered to each other personally. Most church planters and spouses looked forward to those summer retreats, usually held at a camp setting, with child care, meals, and lodging provided.

We also had smaller retreats and training events in regional or local settings. Sometimes we had a singular focus, as when we got pastors and church planters from NYC, Philadelphia, Harrisburg, Baltimore, and D.C. together to focus specifically on urban church issues. I felt honored and privileged to get to know many wonderful pastors and churches from East Coast cities, to share ideas, and to find that our experiences at Diamond Street were not unique. We had much to learn from each other. Those gatherings gave fresh energy and vision to weary urban missioners. The kingdom net was working–and spreading. Joy to the world!

An important dimension of my new assignment was my long involvement with EMM at Diamond Street and with some of the newer churches it had planted in Philadelphia.

I didn't realize at the time that the flurry of EMM church plantings had peaked and would soon slow to more "normal" patterns, as finances tightened, church planters burned out, and we discovered that it was much easier to start churches than to maintain and grow them. Leadership changes at headquarters and in our conference also affected how EMM operated. For example, some of my predecessors made promises, started churches and ministries, only to find as we went along that those rosy promises were not always easy to keep. I felt it was my duty to follow up with a dose of realism where church planters or districts had been promised more than was reasonable. I needed to tread softly, of course, as I also dreamed big dreams and had lofty visions — as expressions of my faith — but I had learned the hard way that vision needs to be tempered by realism. With Paul Landis as President, David Shenk as Overseas Director, Don Jacobs as global consultant, Ervin Stutzman as part of the EMM Home Ministries team and later as Moderator of LMC, there was plenty of visionary activity in that dynamic EMM team! I was humbled to be part of such an experienced group of visionaries.

As is typical for any position with major administrative responsibilities, I spent much of my time in damage control — responding to crises and emergencies. In fact, my role as HM Director seemed to be an on-going balancing act between starting fires and putting them out. Our department tried to ignite evangelism and church planting within traditional churches, often sparking new ideas and ministries. On the other hand, many church plants and new ventures encountered unforeseen difficulties that needed an emergency response. Soon after I began my new role, there was a major crisis in New Orleans, and I got a quick introduction to mediation in church planting. Since I was new to the scene, David Shenk arranged for a Mennonite pilot in Lancaster to fly David and me down to New Orleans quickly. This was one way David could orient me to some current issues and also debrief me on how HM works. I remember the butterflies in my stomach as this small plane flitted up and down across the mountains and around lightning storms, dipping way down near the trees over Harrisonburg, VA, to wave at the pilot's son, who was out working in his yard. Was this going to be my new "normal," being chauffeured in private planes to trouble spots around the country to do damage control? I didn't remember reading that in the job description.

Without getting into the specifics of the New Orleans situation, suffice it to say that Amor Viviente (a Mennonite network of churches in Honduras that had been birthed via EMM) was now planting churches in the US. There were procedural issues among the founders of Amor Viviente, the local church planters, and LMC that needed attention. There were several days of intense meetings as I recall, until an agreement was reached to have one of the couples relocate and let the church planters do their work. I should note here that New Orleans was a great learning experience, but it was rare that I would again take private planes to intervene elsewhere. Perhaps this case was a bit of an overreaction that could have been handled differently. Who knows?

Recruiting, training, and placing church planters took much of our time and energy at HM. It was a complicated process. The first step was usually praying together as a staff about where new churches should be planted. EMM kept maps posted on office walls to show where current churches and church plants were located, or to pray for "empty" spaces on the maps. If we heard about new people groups moving into an area, a natural question was whether any evangelical churches were reaching them. Sometimes, LMC bishops or pastors would approach us with a vision for planting new churches in their region. Places where the Holy Spirit was already nudging people were obvious places to explore.

As Director of Home Ministries, I was often invited to speak at churches or other gatherings. Other HM staff also took speaking engagements. One question I liked to ask churches when I spoke was, "What is the ideal size for a church?" People were often very comfortable in their church and really did not relish growth, because growth meant change. I would say, "As long as some people in your neighborhood have not been reached with the gospel, your church is too small." Herb Miller would hold seminars on "Getting Ready for Company," challenging churches to take active steps to invite their neighbors to church. We also used advertising, posting ads in LMC and EMM publications such as "Church Planters Needed in Boston."

When people responded and came to us to inquire or apply, the next step was screening or vetting. How do you know when someone has a genuine call from God? How were we to "test the spirits"? I recently found several lists of churches planted by EMM over the last sixty years or so and was amazed by their length. I know not all of them exist anymore, but many do, and some have hived off to form their own conferences or networks. Even those that did not last touched many people with the gospel. Nothing done for God is ever in vain. (1 Cor. 15:58) Lasting fruit is not always geographically evident. How many NT churches still exist today?

"We humans make plans, but the Lord has the final word." (Prov. 15:1 CEV) This verse is especially true when planting or growing a church. Paul reminds us that one plants seeds, another waters, but only God can make it grow (1 Cor. 3) when it comes to spiritual agriculture.

It was amazing to watch God at work, giving one person a vision, a second person to confirm, a third person or group to offer resources, and suddenly a new church was born! Often, it would begin with a small-group gathering for Bible study and prayer. As God confirmed the vision, the new young church would grow as people were added, leaders appointed, and buildings found suitable for meetings. New churches often bring contagious excitement; people are eager to see what shape *this new church* in this new location will be like. Newness brings opportunities for change. Statistics show that church planting is one of the most effective ways to spread the gospel and attract new believers. Testimonies and baptisms of new believers are powerful forms of witness to the reality of Jesus and the power of the Holy Spirit to change lives.

New immigrant groups would often find one another, clustering in a receptive section of an East Coast city. The Christians among them would decide they needed a church to anchor their new community. They would then be able to invite new neighbors to come and join them. Christians relocating to other countries often feel displaced and alone. Forming new churches in their own language offers fellowship and community in their new land. Finding fellow believers in this new place brings joy and a sense of family and belonging. Inviting others to join them is a natural impulse. Newly-formed immigrant-specific churches often grew rapidly, adding numbers and diversity to LMC. They also brought the challenge of mutuality and inclusion to us as the host culture. At EMM, we regularly wrestled with how best to grow and include these new churches within our established networks and institutions. Raising and training bilingual young leaders to ensure the church didn't lose its next generation of American-born children and youth presented its own set of problems and promises.

Our two young Chinese churches in Philadelphia illustrate the point. One worships in Mandarin, the other in Cantonese. Lemuel So, former pastor at Love Truth church, would regularly print the Sunday worship bulletin in both Chinese and English, no easy task. For a time, the church preached in one Chinese language while translating into the other, with a third group upstairs watching via closed-circuit TV and someone translating into English for the children and youth or other non-Chinese-speaking visitors. Imagine the task of coordinating that every week! Pastor Lemuel also contacted every Chinese person listed in our city phone book (remember those?) by phone and in newsletters, inviting them to church. Whenever I preached at those churches, I had to cut my sermons in half so a translator could repeat every sentence and still fit within the allotted time.

The young people in both churches also taught me the difference between ABC's and CBC's. CBC's (Chinese-Born Chinese) wanted to preserve the language and customs of the mother country. ABC's (American-Born Chinese), on the other hand, picked up English and American customs in school and in the neighborhoods where they lived. Very sincere and committed young people often felt a call to missions and wanted to worship in English, conduct summer Bible schools in English, and promote short-term mission experiences for the youth. Their parents often told them they had to stay home and take care of their aging parents–their first responsibility–before going off to the mission field. This created real tension in the church. I, as a White overseer, felt ill-prepared and unqualified to mediate in such dilemmas. I loved both groups dearly and wanted to support them in their faith journeys. It called for much prayer and reliance on the Holy Spirit. I was a bridge between the two groups, also between the budding young church and LMC/EMM. An inadequate bridge at best!

Two driving forces fueled all of our work as a mission agency: the Great Commission of Jesus in Matthew 28 and the gathering and scattering of people groups worldwide. The latter has been going on ever since the Tower of Babel; the former, ever since Jesus told us to go into all the world and make disciples.

I will offer a few examples to illustrate how exhilarating and exhausting church planting can be, rather than listing the many new churches EMM has planted.

Hartford, CT, provides an interesting case study. There was a group of young White professionals in the city from Mennonite backgrounds, so they got together, prayed, and targeted one area with a mostly middle-class White population. They got in touch with EMM, and we found a church-planting couple to move up to Hartford to help this group gather people together for a new Mennonite church. Soon they had a few Bible studies going, found a place for Sunday worship services, and got excited about the new church. The young church-planter couple from Lancaster had only agreed to move up there because these five committed couples were already on site and had agreed to serve as the core group for the church plant. That seemed to be so much better than trying to begin from scratch, with no personal relationships on the ground.

Soon, a young Lao immigrant family moved from Bridgeport to Hartford and was advised by their Mennonite friends to check out the new church plant there. Before long, more Lao families followed their lead, moved to Hartford, and joined the new church. Slowly, the original core couples moved away for various reasons, and the young, White church-planter couple was left with the challenge of learning the language and customs of a new immigrant group. The church eventually became a mostly Lao church, although it was located in a White, middle-class area that had been carefully and prayerfully chosen.

A second case study comes to mind. In Birmingham, AL, a citywide church-planting plan was unveiled by several denominations that felt called to join hands to reach the unreached people of the city. Since the city had a sizable African American population, EMM agreed to join the project only if we could find two African American church-planting couples to join the effort with EMM support. We found two such young couples, eager to carry out the Great Commission, and happy to find that EMM would sponsor them. They both had some experience and training, as I recall, and we were overjoyed, since most of the church planters and denominations involved were majority Caucasian. We were very committed to cross-cultural church planting and extending God's call to reach all nations, at home and abroad. So we found a location and the two energetic young couples, both gifted and committed, went to work canvassing the area, starting Bible studies, and looking for a place to meet for worship. We were up and running, eager to see a new young church evolve, with two experienced leadership couples to guide the work.

Unfortunately, the two couples could not work together well and eventually agreed to separate. I can't remember if that resulted in one church, two churches, or no church. While I could trace many details about church plantings and ministry initiatives in various cities and in the Lancaster heartland, those are better chronicled in the records and archives of EMM. Suffice it to say that my life was very busy for those three and a half years. I was happy to try a different "model" by having my office in Philly while connecting remotely to headquarters.

Most of my work flowed in and out of that office as I traveled up and down the East Coast. People from other cities could easily visit me here, rather than find their way to the tiny headquarters in a dot on the map named Salunga, located just off Spooky Nook Road near Lancaster, PA. Our model helped church planters and pastors from other cities feel a little more connected. The gap between EMM and cities may still persist, but attempts to bridge it have been made in various ways over the decades. EMM even moved its headquarters to Hub 450 in downtown Lancaster City, a great step forward in connecting with cities!

Even though the Philly-based office model worked quite well, from my perspective at least, there was a price the HM director would pay over time, no matter where the "home base" was located. That price was the time spent traveling and meeting on the road, being away from home a great deal. It began to wear on me. I loved the people, places, and projects, but the travel and many meetings began to take their toll. Our teenage daughters were asking, "Dad, why are you gone so much of the time? We don't see you very much during the week." That pierced my heart. I did not want to be an absentee father to our daughters in their formative teenage years.

So I was happily surprised one day to get a call at my Philly office from Don Wingert, the director of the Messiah College Philadelphia Campus. He said they were considering starting a new Urban Studies major or minor, and asked whether I would be interested in helping them design the pilot proposal for it. Would I! I felt like God had just dropped another surprise into my lap, and I said yes. When could we meet? The rest is history, as they say, and I'll pick up on that in the next chapter.

CHAPTER 14

Messiah College at Broad and Diamond

That phone call from Don Wingert came sometime in the spring of 1990, I know, because I began working full-time at Messiah's urban campus in the summer of that year. But let me connect the dots.

As I said, I had already taught some of the courses at MCPC, as the Philly Campus came to be known--Messiah College Philadelphia Campus--fondly called simply, "The Philly Campus." Our house was located immediately behind several campus buildings on a side street, so I often went to MCPC to meet with someone. Also, for some time, the Philadelphia SYAS (Mennonite Student and Young Adult Services) office was housed in those buildings, so I often had meetings with various Mennonites there. After several meetings with Don to explore what an Urban Studies major or minor might look like, he dropped another surprise on me. He said, "You know, there is a staff opening here, which you might want to apply for." That position was Director of Student Life, which basically meant overseeing dorm life, along with recruitment and some teaching, among other things. It was a tantalizing idea. (Photo below of Messiah's Philly Campus by Temple U.)

I had no training or experience in college residence life administration, but I did have some experience teaching courses there, as well as in urban pastoring and pastoral counseling. Part of the Student Life Director position also included informal student counseling and serving as a liaison to the counseling staff at the main campus in Grantham, PA. My experience of living and working in the inner city for many years seemed to appeal to the students and staff who interviewed me. After careful, prayerful consideration and several interviews with staff and students at Messiah, I was chosen as the new director. As you might have noticed by now, God seemed to enjoy pushing me into new areas of ministry every so often, areas unfamiliar and untried but somehow seeming to make "sense" in God's amazing grace. This was an answer to prayer after being increasingly troubled by our daughters' question, "Dad, why don't we see you very much these days? Why are you on the road and away from home so often?" Talk about a dramatic change! From traveling up and down the Northeast Corridor almost weekly, to now walking through the back yard (literally!) to my office every day. That was a refreshing and welcome switch.

In 1968, Messiah College and Temple University began a public-private experiment in higher education, the first of its kind in the country. President Ray Hostetter at Messiah and some other forward-thinking educators, such as Ernie Boyer, along with Al Myer of Mennonite Education Association and Manny Ortiz of Westminster Seminary, had decided it might be time to give college students a taste of the city and the offerings of a state university as part of their college education. It was an attempt at better preparing Christian college students for life and service in the real, rapidly urbanizing world. Also, the civil rights ferment of the sixties played into the equation. As the idea grew and locations took shape, President Hostetter and his team decided that Temple was the best fit for Messiah College in establishing this seminal combination. Temple's location and philosophy meshed well with those of Messiah, and the president at Temple was open to the idea. So Messiah bought a few row houses across from Temple, near Broad and Diamond, and renovated them into dorms, offices, and classrooms, launching this unique new venture.

Eventually, Messiah College owned seven four-story townhomes, from 2016 to 2032, on North Broad Street (not including 2020 and 2022), with dorm rooms for up to 80 students, a dining hall and chapel, along with offices, classrooms, a library, a large connecting back yard, and a faculty apartment above the chapel. It was a cozy, secure living-learning arrangement. MCPC students got the best of three worlds: the city, Temple University, and a Christian campus community, all while pursuing a degree in higher education. While remaining at Messiah College, they could choose from hundreds of courses offered by Temple, greatly expanding the range of majors. They were required to take one Messiah course taught by Messiah faculty and to attend our weekly chapel service. In essence, the city became their campus, offering endless experiences not available on a rural campus like Grantham. It was an extraordinary offering, unmatched by other Christian colleges.

Ron Sider was the first dean of the Philly Campus. He and Arbutus moved their young family into the apartment above the chapel, and their boys attended Duckery Elementary, the local public school two blocks away on Diamond Street. (Photo at left shows the Siders revisiting in 2014 as MCPC was about to close.) While Ron was dean of MCPC, he wrote his landmark book, *Rich Christians in an Age of Hunger.* Naomi's brother, Titus Peachey, helped type the manuscript while a student at MCPC and living with us on York Street. Later, Naomi became Ron's office assistant for almost 30 years while he taught at Eastern Baptist Seminary (now Palmer). The Siders also became part of Diamond Street Mennonite Church, just three blocks away, while I was pastor.

The Philly Campus was a highlight of their college experience for many of the approximately three thousand Messiah students who spent a semester or more at MCPC during its 40 years. Several fine histories of Messiah College (now University) have been published. They provide many more in-depth details about the uniqueness of Messiah's satellite campus at Temple. (See especially, *Shared Faith, Bold Vision, Enduring Promise,* by Paul W. Nisly, 2010)

I spent most of that summer of 1990 learning the ropes for my new job, which was multifaceted, to say the least. Learning how to work on a computer, which I had hardly done up until now, took a great deal of time. Instead of dictating my work for several secretaries to transcribe, I now had to get used to doing all my own typing, but also how to do most of my work on a personal computer--all my own on my own desk in my own office--another mind-stretching experience. That meant learning codes, macros, and emails on a network that connected our small campus to the many computers at Grantham, as well as to devices such as printers, copiers, and other high-tech innovations. Networking comes naturally to me, but this was the high-tech kind. The trade-off was well worth it: I could walk home for lunch, and any evening meetings were only a few steps from home, so I could usually enjoy dinner with our family and get to my office and back home in time for a decent bedtime.

The learning curve that first summer was steep. Much time was spent at the computer, learning what Don Wingert told me over and over, "The computer does only what it is told to do!" That was often his response when I would say, "I don't know what's wrong with this stupid computer!" Don was a patient supervisor and knew every nuance of computing, so the learning curve almost turned into a free crash course in computer science. I was glad that I had taught myself to type, first on Grandpa Hostetler's old Remington; later by studying the Sears catalog pictures of keyboards. Now I just needed to learn how to type consistently, manage macros, and use many keys I wasn't used to, such as delete or backspace instead of using White-Out on the printed page. Magical and cool!

I attended various meetings and orientations at the main campus to learn not only how its setup worked but also how it intersected with our campus. I needed to meet the new SLCs (our equivalent to RAs; we had 4, one for each "house" on Broad Street) and plan a week-long orientation with them to prepare for the fall semester. I studied the community ethos covenant statement, which all students had to sign, learning which rules applied particularly to our urban campus, and which were college-wide. Fortunately, those first four SLCs were committed and experienced; they ended up teaching me more than I taught them. Together, we forged a working compact that made us a tight-knit team. We worked together remarkably well that first year. I still consider those four wonderful students lifelong friends and stay connected with them on Facebook. Occasionally, I meet them in person.

I had to order textbooks and write up a syllabus for the class I taught that first year. Most of the classes I taught over the years focused on urban or cross-cultural studies, as well as on various themes in the Bible, urban theology, ethics, and worldviews.

There were several adjustments necessary immediately. First off, Don said my new job required me to live on campus. But since our backyard literally touched the backyard of MCPC's dining hall at 2016-18 N. Broad, Don got the novel idea of removing the fence between us, running a phone line from Messiah to our house, and we'd both agree that I was now "on campus" in a functional, if not actual sense. Of course, this meant I would be on call day and night, in case a student life issue came up and my SLCs needed supervisory help. Or if the fire or burglar alarms went off over there, I'd have to jump out of bed and run over to make sure all procedures were followed. Sometimes it was a false alarm, and the SLCs would call me to say someone had burned toast or a pop tart, and they would handle it. Since the dining hall was open 24/7, it was a popular hangout for students day or night. I could see into the rear dining hall window from our back bedroom windows, so I sort of kept an eye on things all the time anyway. I had to learn fire and police codes, alarm-setting codes, and other specifics about our campus.

I had weekly meetings with the SLCs to ensure we were all on the same page about the ins and outs of Student Life at Messiah College. Much of our work involved orientation, setting clear guidelines (such as dorm room visitation hours), establishing curfews, handling disciplinary cases, and generally keeping the dorms safe and clean. Roommate selection was always a tense time each semester, involving a complicated lottery system.

Pets in rooms were forbidden, except for fish in small aquariums. No candles; fire hazard. Hotplates, irons, and curling irons were carefully monitored. Screens and air conditioners in the windows required special attention, since we were living in century-old brick-and-wood row houses, which posed fire and falling hazards. Those rooms could be breezy in the winter and steaming hot in the summer. For some reason, students were always tempted to crawl out the windows onto the flat roofs, but that was dangerous and forbidden by campus rules. (It is nothing new for college students in Philadelphia to fall off roofs to their death, not only around Temple, but also near other colleges and universities in the city.)

It soon became obvious that while many students came to MCPC for all the right reasons, there were also some who came because they thought they could get away with bending or breaking the rules while roaming the city, things that would get them into trouble back at Grantham. (Drinking, smoking, and dancing were regular temptations.) Fortunately, the SLCs often already knew who those students were and could intervene before things got out of hand.

For a small community of 8 to 10 staff and 60 to 80 students, it took a lot of administrative work to keep everything running smoothly. One of us on staff usually made a run to Grantham on Mondays to take up campus mail, meet with several key staff at the main campus, recruit new Philly students, and maybe attend the weekly faculty meeting. This helped keep the two campuses tightly connected and meshing at key points of intersection. I was often the one making those weekly trips, especially when I was Director of Student Life and/or Recruitment Coordinator. I enjoyed meeting my Student Life peers at Grantham and recruiting prospective students. I even enjoyed attending faculty meetings, which others at the Philly Campus found hard to believe. I'm a teacher at heart, and attending faculty meetings kept me connected to the professors on the main campus.

It also kept me abreast of the educational enterprise, which is, after all, what a college is. I could listen to current issues and debates, as well as hear what academic edges our school was pushing. For years, Messiah's tagline was, "Rigorously Academic, Unapologetically Christian," and as an institution, we lived up to that goal for the most part. Faculty meetings were inspirational for me, helping me connect the classes at Grantham with those in Philly. For several semesters, I taught a Monday evening urban studies class at Grantham, as well as the ones I taught in Philly. Sometimes I arranged field trips to Harrisburg for those Grantham courses. Anything that helped challenge our sheltered

students to engage the city for the sake of Christ's kingdom was ener-
gizing for me, because for me, the urban church was and is key to carrying out the Great Commission in today's urban world. Unless we can
educate our young people to seriously engage the city as residents and
citizens, we will fall far behind in our obligation to make disciples of all
nations.

Running a small campus like ours was complicated because we all
became a team, helping each other as needed, rather than being totally
compartmentalized by department, as was often the case on larger campuses. About half of our staff were Messiah College alumni. Don
Wingert, for example, after graduating from Messiah, was on staff at
Grantham and eventually served as Director of MCPC for many years.
His secretary and assistant, Anne Allen, was a long-term resident of
Philadelphia and a member of Diamond Street Church, where Don,
Andi, and their daughters also attended. So my connections with them
were multifaceted. Others, such as Jane and Douglas Cornman, were
first work-study students at MCPC, then joined the staff after gradu-
ating and rose through the ranks until Jane became Director of Opera-
tions and Douglas Director of Food Services.

Many students who were tentative about coming to the city soon
became very convinced and ardent advocates of the MCPC model for
higher education. They became our best recruiters, sending stories back
to the main campus and getting friends interested in coming. Because
we had a fiber-optic cable connecting our two campuses, students could
call their friends and professors at Grantham by dialing a simple 4-digit
number just as they did back at Grantham. Also, our email systems were
interconnected, making it easy to stay connected. Our students also received Temple accounts and email addresses while here, so they were easily connected to both campuses. Students and parents concerned about
city safety were happy and relieved to have our own cozy, self-contained
campus right across the street from Temple's main campus, with Temple police only a few blocks away and a phone call away. Also, it was re-
assuring that half of our staff lived on campus, including our house and

the two houses on either side of us on Carlisle Street, which were also owned by MCPC. So those fears by new students subsided soon, usually in a few days or at most a few weeks.

One big campus event was a 3-day weekend orientation at the beginning of each semester. I had the SLCs and others help me plan, but it was a huge task: welcoming new students to campus and orienting them to life at MCPC, life at Temple, and life in the big city. It always included a night out in the city with a meal at a downtown restaurant, maybe even a scavenger hunt. Of course, they needed to be taught how to use the SEPTA system, how to buy tokens and transfers, what to do if they got lost, and the many ways not to act like a tourist in their new context. It included several visits to Temple, obtaining Temple ID cards, confirming they were registered for the correct courses, and explaining how to buy textbooks. They had to make sure they had the right roommates and room assignments, understood our food system, knew what to do if they set off alarms, and a million and one details to prepare them for a semester or more with us. Then we had our opening chapel service and began classes. A Temple police officer always came and gave a thorough presentation about safety on and around campus. On the last day of orientation, we always added the returning students to the new group so they would get to know each other. Our students got to know everyone, no matter what their major, which was interesting and often quite different from relationships on bigger campuses.

An added blessing of our urban campus was the availability of city officials and other prominent leaders who would speak in our classes or at chapel services. Philadelphia's first Black mayor, W. Wilson Goode, occasionally spoke in my classes. (Fun fact: since he never came with bodyguards or an entourage, sometimes students at the front desk would not recognize him and not automatically let him in!)

My many years at MCPC, full-time, part-time, and adjunct, over more than 30 years, were some of the richest years of my life. I am still in touch with many former students and staff. The MCPC "family" is real in every sense. Our 40-year review revealed that 20% of our more than

3,000 MCPC alumni still lived within a ten-mile radius of our campus, many inside the city limits. Some are making significant contributions to the city and metro area. As I go through my many files, I find notes of appreciation from students who say my classes or MCPC in general were a highlight of their college experience, often completely reorienting their life principles. Such notes and comments are always encouraging.

I will share a few memories and details about my years at MCPC. I often led a voluntary "Early Christians Bible Study" for students willing to get up at dawn to discuss Bible passages or current issues they were grappling with. College students typically go to bed and get up late, which was a challenge, but it often proved rewarding for those who were really serious about their faith.

I also enjoyed teaching 8:00 a.m. classes since I'm a morning person, and it was easy for me to get up and get there. But it was always interesting to see who would show up in pajamas, come in, spread their bagel or bite into a hot pop tart, and sip fresh coffee. I think it shows who is serious and committed — on some level — if people get up that early and come to class. I know there is a difference, supposedly, between morning persons and night persons, but I think you can change habits with effort. I often told students, "If you want to get ahead in life, get up 30 minutes before other people." That was usually met with groans. I find that my mind is more alert and "fresh" for tasks at hand early in the morning, but maybe that's because I always had to get up at 5 a.m. to feed the chickens and milk the cows when I was a farm boy. Can lifelong habits be set in concrete by age six? Good habits are hard to break.

I often did student counseling, since we didn't have a certified counselor on staff. Having had extensive pastoral counseling experience made me a natural for counseling typical cases that did not involve the most serious issues, which I would need to refer to professionals at the main campus, at Temple, or in the city. Students generally seemed to appreciate my availability, empathy, and respect for their privacy, success, and well-being. I heard many stories, some of which were truly gut-wrenching. If they were life-threatening, of course, I needed to get in touch with my superiors at Grantham.

Many cases involved roommates or boyfriends and girlfriends. I eventually held informal group discussions on male-female relationships, which were always well-attended and rather predictable. By that, I mean girls were ready to commit to a relationship, but guys were not. Or girls wanting open communication and guys holding back. The most fun I remember was teaching a few informal workshops on the book *Men Are from Mars, Women Are from Venus.* That got some great discussions going. I did some informal pre-marriage counseling, but decided I would not perform student weddings, as they needed to do that with their home pastors and churches to be anchored in a faith community. I had enough weddings to do as a minister without adding student weddings. There were a few exceptions, but not many.

Teaching one of my classes at MCPC in 2009.

I met so many wonderful students over the years that I'm a far richer person for having worked there for over 30 years. I could never have imagined the vast network of committed and brilliant young persons eager to learn and serve God who came through the Philly Campus. They came from all over the map, mostly the northeastern parts of the US, but also other parts of the country and the world. It was a joy to have numerous international students, especially after we won the hard-fought right of students from other countries to study at the Philadelphia Campus. In previous years, that was not always possible. Those international students greatly enriched our small campus, and the city enriched their experience in America.

Perhaps you can tell from the wording of that last paragraph that it's hard for me to express some of the complex issues we had to address at MCPC. I won't bore you with too many details, but I must sketch a quick summary of the cross-cultural dilemmas we faced regularly. For years, Calenthia Dowdy and I worked out of adjoining offices in the first-floor hallway of the 2030 building, where students came and went all day, running upstairs to their dorm rooms. I mention that because the locale helps explain the dynamics. That location was at once a hub and a haven, a hub of activity and a haven on the side.

Since Calenthia was an African American from Philly and since she and I often teamed up to teach cross-cultural courses, students of color often came to our corridor and stopped in to vent or share revealing stories. In short, Calenthia and I shared a common conviction that Messiah had a lot of work to do to become a truly multicultural institution where people of color and international students and faculty could all feel equally at home, maximizing their higher education experience. We would often go to the main campus for diversity forums or workshops, put on chapel programs at Grantham and in Philly to highlight our convictions, or meet with small groups of students who were trying to cope with the overwhelming whiteness of most departments at Messiah, including top levels of administration.

The two of us would often come back exhausted and sit in one of our offices to unload, debrief, and exhale. It was exhausting work, and we would look at each other, wondering if it was worth it. The incremental steps of change seemed so small, and the progress so slow, that it felt like a losing battle. Calenthia finally left Messiah to work at Eastern University, perhaps partly out of frustration with the resistance to change at Messiah. I kept leaving and coming back because I had other deep, diverse, and satisfying networks to work with around the city, and also because of my stubborn conviction that the MCPC model was one of the most promising in Christian higher education, refusing to give up on the dream.

I can never thank God and Calenthia enough for those rich years of mutual collaboration. She is a devoted Anabaptist Christian of the highest caliber. I miss those days of working together for the kingdom of Christ. I learned so much from her (and still do). She brought rich personal experiences from growing up Black in North Philadelphia and from working in various ministry settings before coming to MCPC, notably a stint as an officer in the Salvation Army in Camden, NJ, across the river. She went on to earn her PhD and has influenced countless Eastern students in addition to the hundreds she touched at Messiah. She has kept the faith tirelessly, even with the many, many frustrations along the way, and I admire her immensely.

Messiah embraces three faith traditions, which they claim as their founding streams: Anabaptist, Wesleyan, and Pietist. They not only pay lip service, but try to uphold those faiths by making sure you, as a professor, know what they are and that they still value them, while having embraced broad evangelicalism in the classic (not recent) sense. So you were allowed to teach from your faith stance in the classroom, but not to teach against those foundational streams or any other serious biblical tradition that students bring with them. Unless you have experienced it, you cannot imagine the rich, fertile academic soil it has created for the courses I have taught over the years. Any subject, from the Bible to ethics to urban studies to cross-cultural issues, is enhanced by the complex discussions that arise from such a mix of backgrounds.

The issue of pacifism, for example, always generated animated discussions. Students often remarked that late-night bull sessions in dorm rooms revolved around this contentious issue. Some of our students said they had never heard about the peace churches or the peace position till they came to Messiah. Others thought that pacifism was the only viable biblical Christian position possible. You can imagine why these juxtaposed, deeply-held beliefs clashed so vigorously and why they were not easily resolved by late-night discussions, textbook assignments, or classroom lectures.

Nothing shapes or reshapes your religious convictions quite like testimonies from fellow believers whom you deeply respect. More than a few students came to me after class or in my office or over dining hall conversations with comments such as, "Freeman, do you think I'm a heathen if I hold to the just-war theory? I come from a family with a long military history, and my father would disown me if I became a pacifist." Or, "I find the biblical arguments for pacifism very compelling, but I don't know how to talk about it at my home or home church without facing the wrath of my community. What shall I do?" You can imagine the challenge this creates for a Mennonite pastor/professor! How do you advise such sincere young believers on their journey of a lifetime? How do you hold their inherent beliefs and your own in a dynamic tension that the Holy Spirit can use to help both of you grow your faith?

There were many other subjects that created similar fertile dilemmas. Take racism for one more specific case; students would make comments like, "I don't know what to do when I go home for the holidays. My grandpa is such a racist! How do I confront his racism while still loving him as my grandpa?" Or take the idea of embracing the city not only as a viable human habitat but even a key to spreading the gospel. "I am a country boy at heart, but I'm beginning to love the idea of living in the city. I don't know how to tell my girlfriend or my parents. They would think I lost my mind." Tread softly but boldly into your brave future, young man!

And so it went, year after year, as I moved from one office to another (literally; I had at least six different offices in my years at MCPC) or from position to position, both part-time and full-time. The memories pile up rich and deep even as I reflect back and write about them. I would not trade those years for the world. I had many great experiences on both campuses, both Grantham and Philly. I marvel that God saw fit to let me be part of one of the greatest experiments in Christian higher education. When I read the history of the Philadelphia Campus in various books and articles, I couldn't believe that Messiah's administration said after 40 amazing years that the model was "no longer sustainable." How so? When Messiah began even whispering about closing the Philly Campus, the 3,000-plus alumni rose up with a "No Way! You cannot close it. That was one of the best parts of my entire college experience!"

After years of contentious discussion, the decision was made to sell the buildings to Temple and focus on a smaller urban presence in nearby Harrisburg. And to think that at one time there was serious conversation about building the Philadelphia Campus into a full-blown, four-year college, filling an entire city block, recruiting African American students and other minorities from North Philadelphia and across the city! I could hardly contain my surprise and disappointment when I read those discussions in the various histories. But don't get me started. You can't change the past.

CHAPTER 15

Turning into a Bishop

The next new turn in the road for me came in the early 90's when Bishop Luke Stoltzfus began talking about retirement. There were several years of planning and processing among the credentialed ministers in the Delaware Valley District of LMC, which ultimately led to the division of the district into three new districts: South Jersey, the Chester region (Delaware Valley South), and Philadelphia. After all options were weighed and prayed through, I was chosen by consensus to become the new bishop of Philly, with ordination in 1994, followed by a one-year overlap with Luke as he phased out and I phased in. This turned out to be a well-planned succession process, which I applaud Luke for initiating. He had the foresight to realize that the district's incredible growth would remain strong only if he carefully handed off oversight in ways that allowed the new bishops to prepare and the congregations to accept and own the changes. The many years of Luke's faithful service could have turned to upheaval and uncertainty if he had suddenly announced his retirement and moved away.

Richard (Dick) Landis was chosen to oversee the churches in southern New Jersey. Leon Schnupp became the new bishop of the Chester region just south of Philadelphia, and I was tasked with overseeing the dozen or so churches in Philadelphia.

Of course, this meant juggling various pieces of my life, so I ended up working part-time at MCPC and part-time as a bishop. Diamond Street church remained our home church, where we kept our membership, even as we began regular visits to the other churches in my charge. I created quarterly church-visitation schedules and distributed them to the district pastors so they would know when to expect us and where we would be on the other Sundays when they didn't see me. This was my way of treating each church alike and avoiding "favorites," where we attended more often. It was also a unifying device. The smaller, newer churches received the same attention as the more established ones; at the same time, the older ones were aware of the newer ones and shared in our Philadelphia District church life together.

I not only visited the churches for Sunday services but also met one-on-one with the pastors. This often meant meeting at the pastor's office (if they had one), at my office, or at a restaurant for lunch or breakfast. Deep friendships and spiritual partnerships developed from this arrangement, which I treasure to this day. Staff and students at Messiah thus became used to seeing pastors come to my office or even speak in my classes. For the most part, this was a great arrangement, as it introduced students to the rich ethnic and international diversity of our churches and their leaders.

Sometimes I hosted district meetings at MCPC, which also introduced our churches to Messiah College and its urban presence. For several years, I also hosted the monthly breakfast meetings for all Anabaptist pastors in the city (known as "Kingdom Builders Anabaptist Network") on campus, which was very convenient. Messiah allowed us to use their dining room amenities, including coffee, juice, and other beverages, along with the pastries we provided. Once again, I was amazed at how God puts the pieces of one's life and ministry together. Ideas that were once inconceivable became everyday realities.

I arranged with MCPC to have my office serve not only as my Messiah College office but also as the office where our pastors could drop in for visits. That was a real blessing, as I didn't have to run to several different offices to juggle the various parts of my work. One drawback was the lack of adequate parking at MCPC, so sometimes I met with pastors across the street at McDonald's, which had a parking lot.

I had a hard time thinking of myself as a bishop.

I had lived in the city long enough and had watched Luke adapt and modify his position on issues — even on divorce and remarriage — along the way. I had also worked with other LMC bishops as Director of Home Ministries at EMM, both in urban and rural settings, so I learned from observing them what worked well and what to avoid.

I remember telling my Urban Studies professor at Temple that I had become a bishop. He wanted to know if I wore the bishop's costume. When I told him Mennonite bishops don't wear distinctive garb, he was disappointed. He said, "Oh, I like those funny pointed hats!" I also worked with people from many backgrounds in our churches. Some who came from a Roman Catholic background did not have the best view of bishops, and I had to explain carefully how Mennonite bishops differ from those in other traditions. As I tried to explain my role, I sometimes likened it to that of a Methodist bishop, who was a kind of supervisor for a district, but I had to clarify that I did not have authority to move pastors around every five years, as is their custom. Nor was I like an AME bishop, who candidated for his appointment almost like U.S. presidents and mayors did before elections. Sometimes I said I was a "pastor to the pastors" in our district. No definition seemed fully adequate.

In my new role as bishop, I especially enjoyed watching new churches being planted in the city and helping them grow, adapt, choose leaders, ordain pastors, craft clear mission statements, and bring new believers into the body of Christ. I enjoyed the challenge of learning new languages, customs, and foods of the various new immigrant congregations joining our district. An even greater challenge was getting the churches to know and appreciate one another. The New Testament model of all the churches in one city serving and witnessing as one had a lofty allure but was notoriously difficult to emulate. Each ethnic group or nationality brings its customs and rituals, only to find they must adapt to new locations and contexts. From Pentecost to Philadelphia, maintaining the "unity of the Spirit" is a spiritual exercise that stretches and enlarges the church as the Holy Spirit leads.

To illustrate, let me give a few examples. George Kuttab, our Palestinian Mennonite pastor, would eagerly insist that people try the delicious Middle Eastern cuisine his wife had prepared, but he himself was reluctant to try food from a country he was not familiar with. So I said that for oneness in the body of Christ we needed to respect and try each other's favorite dishes, worship styles, and family traditions. Brother George grinned, groaned, and grew, right along with the rest of us. Taking off my shoes to preach at the Indian church was new for me, but it made perfect sense. It made me feel they were more biblical than I was.

Kneeling for long periods of prayer was a deeply ingrained and meaningful tradition that was hard on my knees and almost impossible after my knee replacement. Singing in English or a different mother tongue, with or without instruments, from hymn books or "off the wall," singing and clapping loudly or sitting in reverent silence--these all presented both opportunities and challenges, as you can well imagine. But it led to important stretching and growth toward the NT church and the future church of Revelation 7. As we laughed and cried along the way, learning from each other, we all discovered that no one has a monopoly on God's people or the one best set of traditions. As iron sharpens iron, so culture sharpens culture.

Our Philadelphia District sometimes had as many as 15 churches (including two in Hawaii), often with 10 or more language groups, including Chinese (Mandarin and Cantonese), Vietnamese, Cambodian (Khmer), Lao (Hmong), Indonesian, Spanish, English, Arabic, and several Nigerian languages. New churches often started in homes, and some remained "house" churches. More typically, they grew until they could rent or buy their own buildings for worship and outreach. All of them struggled financially because they were mostly located in inner-city areas. Most of the pastors were bi-vocational. This presented a unique challenge with some of the Asian churches, as especially Chinese pastors had strongly-held beliefs that only fully-trained, fully-supported, full-time pastors qualified for ordination. Of course, that did not fit well with our Anabaptist tradition of ordaining pastors with or without seminary training.

Philadelphia District leadership meeting, January, 1999.

My least favorite task as bishop was to help settle church problems, of which there were more than a few. I sometimes asked God if the church really was his idea or if he had any second thoughts. But I was reassured by the Holy Spirit and the witness of scripture when I recalled that Jesus said, "I will build my church and the gates of hell will not prevail against it." It was also a good reminder that we humans do not build the church; we are merely the instruments God uses. I felt fortunate that God would consider using me in such a global enterprise. God showed up over and over along the way, often in ways no human could have envisioned or engineered. I won't go into many details about the various church problems, only to say that sometimes I had to call in other bishops to help solve the seemingly unsolvable. When cross-cultural traditions complicated matters, I often had to ask others from that culture for help. Many cups of black coffee and discussions into the night were needed, but God always made a way when there seemed to be no way.

A quick example: one Asian church asked me to please help their pastor retire and relocate so they could choose a new pastor. Meanwhile, the pastor asked me to help the elders find a new pastor so he could retire! The elders thought that would be an insult to their founding pastor, who was their spiritual father.. What was a Caucasian bishop to do with this intercultural conundrum? God helped find a way through some very creative elders.

Of course, East versus West was often involved when it came to immigrant churches. I just discovered a gem of a book last week (I'm writing this on Memorial Day 2019) that I had on my shelf but apparently forgot about for 20 years, which spoke to one of those issues. I'm enjoying the book now and wish I'd had time to read it then! The title is *Following Jesus Without Dishonoring Your Parents,* (IVP, 1998), written by a team of young Asians involved in ministry with Intervarsity Christian Fellowship. They struggle valiantly with various scriptures that call for putting faithfulness to Christ above family and culture, but they also wrestle with the Asian tradition that places loyalty to family above all else. I remember some of the dear young Asians in our churches telling me from time to time that they felt called to ministry or missions, but their parents would be crushed if they did not get a good education, a respectable profession and income, and then take care of their parents until the parents died. How should a Caucasian Mennonite bishop advise such sincere, committed young Christians caught between several cultures? The book is excellent and timely.

Instead of trying to describe each of the many wonderful churches and people I got to work with, I will give a brief thumbnail sketch of a few of them to give readers a taste of what my life was like during those rich and meaningful years. (I was active in my bishop role for 15 years, from 1994 to 2009.) I will try an alphabetical listing to keep things simple. [Note: A fuller description of these churches can be found in *All God's Children; a history of Lancaster Conference churches in Philadelphia,* a book written in 2000 by Miriam Stoltzfus and Jeff Gingerich to chronicle the first 100 years of mission work and church planting by

LMC in our great city. A committee of us helped gather information and photos to give brief sketches of each church, a ready reference for anyone who wants more details. Several copies are housed in the archives and library of Lancaster Mennonite Historical Society in Lancaster, PA, now known as "Mennonite Life."]

<u>Abundant Life Chinese Mennonite Church </u>in South Philadelphia, located at Broad and Moore Streets, is an amazing church that has touched hundreds of neighbors with the love of Christ for many years and has raised up leaders for the church and for missions around the world. It was one of the three Asian churches started by Ted Yao, an engineer from China who relocated to Lancaster and eventually to Philadelphia. Ted loved the Lord and could not help himself. He shared his faith in Jesus, his Lord and Savior, with those around him and began Bible studies that later grew into churches. Ted did not seem to have the gifts for long-term pastoring, but handed off his fledgling believer groups to other leaders to serve as pastors while he continued his ministry elsewhere. I doubt that we will ever know how many people Ted led to faith in Jesus, nor how many churches he started around the world, till we get to the other side and see God open all the books. Ted was unassuming and humble, always concerned that every language group he worked with would have its own church in its own language, led by gifted leaders. I didn't realize that Ted was an engineer until I read his obituary! Apparently, he was quite the businessman in several Asian countries and in America. Ted is one of the many global saints I learned to know in my improbable life journey.

Abundant Life church purchased a 3-story, large corner rowhouse, formerly a business with display windows on Broad Street and also on Moore Street. They used every inch of space almost every day of the week, holding language classes (English and Chinese), summer camps, VBS, neighborhood projects, and distributing hundreds of copies of the *Chinese Christian Herald* each month when it was published. It connects millions of Christians around the world and lets them know they are not alone, but part of a growing network of Christ's kingdom.

We enjoyed the dynamic worship (contemporary praise and traditional hymns in both English and Chinese), the warm fellowship, and, especially, the delicious Chinese meals after church each Sunday, as they packed everyone into the tiny basement for both physical and spiritual nourishment. The hospitality of Asian people is unmatched.

Abundant Life usually wanted me to preach on my quarterly visits, and I often did, but I also wanted to experience their church as it is when we're not there. It is incredible to watch how hard they work to print bulletins, prepare overheads, and interpret every aspect of their life together in three languages: Cantonese, Mandarin, and English. There were also often Indonesians or other Asians who came to join them. It was not unusual for someone to quietly interpret into yet another language in a corner somewhere. They were very receptive to my sermons, often begging me to come more often, but it was challenging to preach with two interpreters repeating every sentence. It is difficult to retool a 30-minute sermon to fit into a 45-minute space where everything is explained three times, and you hope the meaning is clear in each of those receptor groups.

Many members at Abundant Life were first-generation immigrants, but they also had an army of young people, second- and third-generation folks who often excelled in computer science or other high-tech trades. They helped me understand the big differences between ABCs and CBCs— American Born Chinese versus Chinese Born Chinese. My earlier comments alluded to the tension between parents who want to preserve the best of the old country and those who want their children to have a good American education and a quality professional income.

These dear young people have to juggle the American dream with the traditions brought over from Asia, then sort through those competing value systems under the new set of values brought by the gospel and the teachings of Christ. It's such a gift to be allowed to walk alongside these families as they try to make sense of it all. It's fair to say that we learned more than they did in the process. It makes passages such as Revelation 7 come alive in brand new ways. Now, when I think of the multitude from every tribe and nation around God's throne, I can imagine myself singing and dancing (maybe by then I'll know how!) beside Truong Tu or Benny Lee!

<u>Bethany House of Worship</u> was an unusual case. Pastor Sanjeevarao Vangore was the son of a Mennonite pastor in India, so when he came to the U.S. he wanted to stay connected to the Mennonite Church. As a substitute teacher in the Philadelphia school system, he witnessed to others from India and Pakistan, leading some of them to the Lord. Then he started Bible studies, and they wanted him to be their pastor. I think somehow Luke Stoltzfus and Jim Leaman got to know him and eventually arranged for them to use the Oxford Circle church building on Sunday afternoons for services, and Luke arranged for Vangore to be licensed for ministry in the Lancaster Conference. So the church was never officially an LMC church, but Vangore was the pastor with an LMC license, and we treated them as part of us. At one point, the church leaders held a vote but decided not to join LMC as a congregation. The arrangement worked well as long as Vangore was alive and serving as pastor. When he died, the congregation stayed independent.

After the church grew to about 50 to 60 people, they bought a building in the Olney section of Philadelphia and renovated what had been a synagogue, as I recall. They were a very devout group, with solemn worship services held entirely in Hindi. When I visited them, sometimes they wanted me to preach; at other times, I simply brought greetings or a prayer. They all removed their shoes when they entered the sanctuary, and spent a long time on their knees praying softly before the rest of the service. After announcements, singing, and scripture readings, the pastor would preach a lengthy sermon in Hindi, with some English sprinkled in for visitors like us. As I recall, my sermons in English were not translated, so it seems most people understood English quite well. Most of them seemed to be first-generation immigrants, with some amazing stories of miracles and salvation. As I said, I always removed my shoes to preach, and they listened with deep reverence.

<u>Christian Life Mennonite Church</u> was begun in the East Falls neighborhood by Parker and Anna Mavis, who came from South Africa via California and Fuller Seminary. Pastor Mavis had a vision to start a more middle-class church in a growing African American neighborhood to reach those moving up and out of the inner city. This was to be a self-sustaining church, rather than the "mission churches" that Mennonite church planters had begun in low-income neighborhoods in the past. Eventually, some Whites also joined the effort, and it seemed appropriate that a "colored" post-apartheid pastor from Johannesburg should lead such an effort at establishing a racially integrated Mennonite church in Philadelphia. For a while, the church attracted people with this vision, especially those living in the East Falls section of the city, some of whom had connections to other Mennonite churches in the area. Diamond Street Church even supported the church plant, and several people from the church joined Mavis in starting it. James and Kathleen Dennis, along with Gunsalla and Bea Macon, were among those from Diamond Street who went to help.

After Parker and Anna returned to South Africa to continue the ministries they had established there before coming to the US, the church voted to appoint James Dennis as their new pastor. James and

Kathleen still lived in North Philadelphia but commuted faithfully to the small church until it closed when they retired and moved to Georgia.

The church met in a small Seventh-day Baptist church building, a great arrangement because the Baptists worshipped on Saturdays and the Mennonites on Sundays. Worship services were rather informal, sometimes starting slowly or late, but they picked up with some animated singing, often led by Beatrice Macon. Bea and Gunsalla Macon lived in the area, so it made sense for them to attend there. The singing was a blend of Black gospel and old-style Southern Black hymns, sometimes with piano accompaniment, depending on whether someone could play. There was clapping and plenty of amens, with dynamic testimonies of how God was working in people's lives. It turned into a mostly Black congregation, with a smattering of others at times. The church bought a van, which Brother James kept polished and shiny, parked during the week in Sam Kuttab's large warehouse on Broad Street. They would pick up people for service and midweek Bible studies, some of whom were older or had disabilities.

Pastor James Dennis preached powerful biblical sermons, encouraging people to give their all to following Jesus. He preached from the Bible, used many personal illustrations, and challenged people to deepen their walk with God and to share their faith during the week. People loved their pastor, and he loved the people he shepherded, calling them, visiting them in the hospital, and making sure he cared for each of them no matter what they were going through. He tried several times to assemble a pastoral team, but no permanent team formed.

James Dennis was a walking miracle, whose story has been told elsewhere, but I need to mention here that he used to hate White people because of all he and his family suffered in the South, where he grew up. He had hoped to kill at least one White man, and almost did, spending time in prison for the effort. It was in prison that I first met him, and after his release, he, Kathy, and their entire family joined us at Diamond Street. James and I are very close friends, and I believe we would be willing to die for each other if the need arose. God did a great miracle in both of us, creating such a tight bond of brotherhood, and we went through all kinds of ministry challenges together. His story could fill another book, a book that would be well worth reading. After they retired and moved to Georgia, they left a big hole in the neighborhood and in our hearts. Every time we talk by phone, it's just like picking up where we left off yesterday. Here is a cover photo of James and me chatting in my office in 1989.

Even though Christian Life closed its doors, it never closed its heart. The group of believers there is still bound together in spirit, even if they are now scattered. Our family and the Dennis family are still very close, even though we don't see each other very often. Naomi and I spent a delightful weekend with them in their southern home.

Diamond Street Mennonite Church has been described in detail elsewhere, so I won't say much about it here, except to note that it underwent leadership changes and began to decline. Eventually, it merged with another church and moved farther north on Broad Street. Its long history bore much Kingdom fruit, which continues to this day. I wrote a summary titled "Whatever Happened to Diamond Street?" that appeared in the November 2012 issue of the magazine *The Mennonite.*

Ethiopian Evangelical Church of Philadelphia had an interesting history dating back to West Philadelphia Mennonite, when a young Eastern University student from Ethiopia attended and felt a burden to start an evangelical witness to the many Ethiopians in the city. Yeshitala Mengistu helped get the group started through Bible studies and fellowship events, which ultimately led to the church being situated in a chapel in University City. Later, it moved to the 69th Street Alliance Church on the city's edge in Upper Darby. Under the robust leadership of Pastor Endalkachew Salih Ayo and his famous singer-wife Bethlehem Woldi, the church flourished until Pastor Endalks moved to pastor a large Ethiopian church in Silver Spring, MD. A few followed him or may visit that church occasionally, but most are scattered and no longer meet regularly as a church in Philadelphia. Aslaku Berhanu, my good friend and colleague who works for the Blockson Collection at Temple, sadly informed me of this when I was asking her in 2018 about the church and the pastor. She was a long-standing and devout member there.

So here is another somewhat sad ending to a vital evangelical church that touched many persons with the gospel over the years. It was always hard for Naomi and me to worship there, because they would do everything in Amharic, until someone would whisper into my ear that it was time for me to get up and preach, bring greetings, or whatever else the bishop was supposed to do on this visit. Sometimes, Aslaku or another kind member would sit beside us and write a few notes in English to give us a hint about what was being said or sung.

The prayers and singing were very upbeat, deeply spiritual, and contagious. Without understanding a word, you could tell that these dear people loved the Lord and believed in deep worship. The mood of their services was deep devotion and exuberant praise. A highlight of the singing was the occasional eruption of the high female "la la la la" (my poor English attempt at spelling the unspellable) in an angelic voice in the middle of a song that seemed like a bird taking off for heaven. The sermons were peppered with quiet "amens" or other verbal affirmations of truth being proclaimed. Most of their services began with everyone on their knees, offering soft prayers, sobs, or murmurs of praise, often for 20 to 30 minutes before the organized service began. (This became impossible for me after my knee replacement.) As with so many of the immigrant churches, I often felt challenged and rebuked by how shallow our Western ways of worship seemed in comparison to theirs. The vibrancy and sincerity of these saints from other shores were palpable and transcendent. You knew you were in a house of worship and in the presence of a holy God. We learned a lot from them.

<u>Oxford Circle Mennonite Church</u> had a history almost as long as that of Diamond Street; in fact, both of them grew out of Norris Square Mennonite, the first LMC church plant in the city. After Norris Square transitioned into a Spanish congregation, Arca de Salvacion, some English-speaking members went to Oxford Circle, which had begun as an outreach to children and families living in Oxford Village, a housing project in the lower Northeast part of the city. Eventually, they built a church at the corner of Langdon and Howell Streets. For many years, this church was led by several sister workers and lead pastor Jim Leaman. For years, members of LMC churches in the country would come into the city to help, but eventually it became a self-sustaining city church.

When Leonard Dow became the first African American pastor in 1999, the church became a community-focused church, beginning many outreach programs to help improve the living conditions in the neighborhood, from childcare to ESL classes, to job creation and training, to food-distribution, to working with local public schools, all as efforts to share the love of God more broadly in the neighborhood.

The church established a nonprofit organization, Oxford Circle Christian Community Development Association (OCCCDA, or simply OC3), to more effectively carry out these many outreach programs. Its governing board consists of church and community members. It moves the church beyond its four walls and invites people inside them. Every fall, there is a community festival celebrating the end of summer and the beginning of the new school year. Neighbors are fed, entertained, and connected to local resources. Some neighbors have become church members. Pastor Leonard used to ask, "If we love the people in Oxford Circle, how will they know?" OC3 became a robust, multifaceted ongoing solution.

As the church became more multicultural, it chose to redefine itself as a holistic, community-focused Anabaptist church, pioneering new ways of relating to urban diversity and promise. Eventually, they bought a campus diagonally across the street, still at Langdon and Howell Streets, where they have several buildings and a large fenced-in parking lot. Numerous church families live in the surrounding community and have become "incarnational" in the area, becoming part of the local social fabric while aiming to be the salt, light, and yeast Jesus talked about, reflecting his image on earth and continuing his work. Multicultural pastoral and leadership teams are leading the way toward oneness in Christ with various ethnic and international "flavors." Oxford Circle Mennonite Church is the most ethnically diverse Mennonite church in the city today. The current pastoral team is Pastors Lynn Parks, Ron Tinsley, Lyllian Velazquez, and JoEl Rohrer.

<u>Vietnamese Mennonite Church</u> in Southwest Philadelphia has had a rich and varied history, located at the corner of Woodland and 63rd Streets. They bought an old vacant four-story club building, renovated it, and have planted various daughter churches inside and outside the city. Services in Vietnamese and English have led to several English-speaking churches and various outreach programs in the area. For years, the able leadership of founding pastor Quang X. Tran led to continuous growth and a vibrant community of faith. Later, Pastor/Bishop Tuyen Nguyen raised up many young leaders through the STEP program and helped plant daughter churches in the U.S. and new Mennonite churches in Vietnam. It has been a great joy to watch the able teams of leaders effectively spread the love of Jesus among Vietnamese immigrants and many other seekers. For several years, I had my bishop's office at VMC and hosted numerous district meetings there. We had a district council (made up of various pastors) that met there and helped oversee new and existing church plants.

This is not a complete list of the churches I worked with as bishop, but it is a representative sampling. More extensive records and histories exist elsewhere, in LMC bishop board minutes, EMM reports, and in

the archives of Lancaster Mennonite Historical Society (now Mennonite Life). As mentioned, a one-book summary of the history of these
and other churches was published in 2000, written by Miriam Stoltzfus and Jeff Gingerich under the title *All God's Children.* My bishop
work also involved leading and participating in other networks, such
as the Philadelphia Mennonite Council (now Kingdom Builders Anabaptist Network of Greater Philadelphia), and city-wide groups such
as the Evangelical-Catholic Dialogue, along with Ron Sider. At times,
it stretched my Amish/Mennonite soul rather far, but also greatly enriched it.

The longer I lived and served in Philadelphia, the more convinced I
became that the multicultural expression of the urban church is a chosen vessel that God is using to expand the Kingdom of Christ around
the world. I was privileged to experience that same expression in other
cities such as Honolulu, Manila, Singapore, Hong Kong, Phnom Penh,
Ho Chi Minh City, Cape Town, Lokoja, Nairobi, and others. Many
of these cities I visited as Fraternal Representative to Asia for LMC, a
role that took me to Southeast Asia on several trips to strengthen relationships between LMC/EMM and the churches we helped plant in
other countries. At first, LMC thought of them as "daughter churches,"
but after they matured and became self-sustaining, they became "sister
churches," with much to teach us.

On my first trip to Asia, for example, Howard Witmer and I, as
LMC bishops, helped churches in the Philippines ordain their first four
bishops. After that, they ordained their own bishops. On another trip,
Carl Horning, a fellow LMC bishop, and I ordained pastors for the two
churches in Hawaii, which were part of the Philadelphia District. The
Asian churches were always warm, receptive, and vibrant; we learned
a great deal from them. This is an exciting time to be alive, to witness
Christ building his global church as a precursor to the new heavens
and new earth, where we will experience things we could only dream of
here and now. I always came back from those trips, excited and encouraged, wanting our Western churches to become more like them. They

are sending missionaries to other countries now, including the United States. What an exciting full-circle moment in church history!

CHAPTER 16

Reflections Upon Retiring

It is not easy deciding when to retire. Tee, one of my amazing sons-in-law, keeps reminding me that I might represent the last generation of Americans to have the luxury of considering retirement. Perhaps the economic realities of the future will no longer allow older citizens to stop working, collect Social Security, and live without a constant, steady income from gainful employment. Time will tell.

The LMC Bishop Board had a very sensible retirement policy, I thought. When a bishop turned 65, he needed to begin implementing a retirement plan. By age 70, he was to have completed the process of handing over his duties as bishop to a younger person or team. So I began to act accordingly. In 2009, after 15 years as bishop, I handed over to a younger team of bishops at age 67. There had been several years of preparation for the transition, as the pastors of the district and I worked through the realities of our young urban collection of churches versus the realities of the LMC bishop model. The LMC model assumed that one bishop could effectively oversee a geographic region of established churches, which in turn could support their pastors and contribute to a fund for bishops' support. That model was not sustainable in Philly, where our churches could barely support their own pastors, let alone a bishop. That is one reason I always worked part-time jobs alongside my bishop work. Naomi's work for Ron Sider also contributed significantly to our household budget.

So the Lord helped us move to a team model, where we subdivided the district into four quadrants, with one pastor in each quadrant joining a bishop team without leaving their pulpit. The idea was that their churches could support them as before, and they could take on some part-time bishop work alongside their pastoral duties, while surrounding themselves with a team of leaders at their respective churches. This way, they could each oversee churches in their respective areas and coordinate a team approach to overseeing one another's churches as well. They could take turns representing the Philadelphia District at Bishop Board meetings, would not need to travel as far or as often, and would retain their health and other benefits through their pastoral support packages at their respective churches. This seemed like a real answer to prayer and also opened the door to a new, multicultural model of an urban bishop team. Excitement and enthusiasm ran high, and I felt relieved to hand over to four very gifted younger men. Here is a photo of the ordination/commissioning service.

In 2009, I handed over my responsibilities as bishop to Leonard Dow, Tuyen Nguyen, Al Motley, and Tim Darling. This was a team of two African Americans, an Asian American, and a Caucasian American. They clicked as a team, and we had wonderful team meetings as I met with them to begin transitioning out as they transitioned in to take on the oversight of the district.

Even though I had gradually disengaged from various boards and committees (such as the Philadelphia Mennonite High School board and the Eastern Mennonite Missions board), I remained partially engaged in a few things, including teaching at Messiah College's Philadelphia Campus until it closed around 2014. Even after it closed, I served as liaison between Messiah and Temple as five students needed an extra semester of Temple credit. I was happy to shed many of my administrative burdens, but found out that one cannot so easily dismiss from one's heart the relationships one has carried there with passion for many years. There were always weddings, funerals, anniversaries, and other events at our district churches that vied for my ongoing attention, even though I was no longer officially "responsible" for them.

The rest of this last chapter may not feel entirely congruent, as it was written at different times and places (while we were living on Carlisle Street, or later, on Discher Street). Some are general reflections, some describe actual events, some were culled from my various journals or notebooks. That helps explain why I might change from first person to third person, present tense to past tense, depending on where and when it was written. I hope this patchwork arrangement will not be too disorienting. Don't try too hard to make all the pieces fit; after all, the pieces of my life have never fitted neatly into organized categories, as you well know by now.

The first day of my retirement (July 1, 2009), I went to Pennsylvania Hospital for hernia surgery. It seemed like a good time to take care of a problem that wasn't exactly pressing, but might become so eventually. Dr. Honish, our long-time family doctor, and my surgeon made it seem so simple, since it was now done with minimally invasive laparoscopic technology. The surgeon assured me that he had done thousands of these procedures and they were boringly routine. Nothing to worry about. Accordingly, I went in on July 1, knowing they would give me general anesthesia and that Naomi would be there with me, even though they said she could go to work after dropping me off, then come back to pick me up after work, when I had recovered from my anesthesia.

The "boring routine" turned out to be anything but.

I ended up in the ER and stayed in the hospital for nine days, almost losing my life. I'm so glad Naomi did NOT go into work, that she was there to ask questions and be present as I was in and out of awareness, not sure what was going on. Dr. Honish later told us he was sure they nicked an artery during the surgery, which led to internal bleeding, which they eventually discovered and finally stopped after various transfusions and procedures. The surgeon denied any error on his part, although one of his assistants seemed to agree that a tiny blood vessel had somehow begun bleeding, and they eventually stopped it.

The most frustrating part was that the surgeon did not communicate with Naomi or keep her in the loop about what was going on. She had to constantly press nurses and others for answers as my life hung in the balance. I was never more grateful for my loving, serving, persisting darling soulmate than in those tenuous days. Every time I was on the verge of despair or unsure of where I was, this glowing angel would walk into my room, and the clouds would lift. She was a heavenly ray of sunshine every day, and I can never thank her enough for hanging in there with me in those dark days.

We later learned that July 1 is the worst day of the year for surgery, as new interns begin training with surgeons on that day, marking the start of a new cycle. We also learned from the surgeon during a subsequent visit that Naomi did not complain loudly enough (he used more colorful language) to get his attention. She replied that she should not have had to pester him for him to communicate with her. We also found out that surgeons do not necessarily have the best bedside manners with patients, and are often referred to as "carpenters" by other medical staff; that is, technicians who use their tools but don't always have "the human touch." I finally regained my strength and went home to retire and continue healing. That was a close call.

Another topic worth mentioning is the popular notion that "retirement isn't biblical." Especially among Black churches, one often hears the common adage that "The man of God does not retire!" Indeed, I've known of African American pastors literally dying in the pulpit while preaching--from heart attacks or utter exhaustion. Some even told me, "White pastors burn out; Black pastors just burn up!" So there was the burden of race on top of theology. I knew I was exhausted from years of stressful multitasking as a minister, overseer, teacher, community leader, husband, father, and other roles, with no sabbaticals along the way (except for one brief summer break). I needed a change of pace or face the real possibility of ruining my health.

In my struggle to make sense of it all, I began my own research into what the Bible actually said, if anything, about retirement. I was astonished to find out that in Numbers 8, God had given Moses very specific instructions about priests and their age requirements. He specifically said they could not serve as priests before age 25 and that they needed to retire at age 50! They could still assist younger priests, but not be in charge. Here is the quote:

23 The Lord said to Moses, 24 "This applies to the Levites: Men twenty-five years old or more shall come to take part in the work at the tent of meeting, 25 but at the age of fifty, they must retire from their regular service and work no longer. 26 They may assist their brothers in performing their duties at the tent of meeting, but they themselves must not do the work. This, then, is how you are to assign the responsibilities of the Levites." (Num. 8:23 - 26)

Wow! Where were all the preachers, theologians, and holy pundits during my lifetime, that I had never heard any sermons on this text? I ended up writing an article about it, which *The Mennonite* magazine published in 2012 (right next to an article about a pastor who had served 50 years). Even though that text refers explicitly to leaders of God's flock, the principle itself makes sense. Leaders often hang on too long, when it would seem much wiser to train younger leaders, phase them into service, assist them, and gradually let them take over as you take on less and less. Even John the Baptist knew this when he said about Jesus, "He must increase, and I must decrease." How profound! This assures stability and sustainability in kingdom work. So now I could rest easy in my soul as I began choosing which things to take on and which to let go.

I need to clarify: those who say retirement is not biblical may mean something much narrower than retirement itself. They may mean that the popular image of retired folks doing nothing but golfing, eating, swimming, and traveling the world without a care or responsibility–that popular *image* of retirement–is not biblical. They have a point. I essentially agree with them here. I believe that followers of Jesus never stop serving the Lord in ways appropriate to their gifts and abilities. We are to be witnesses for Jesus and call others to follow him all the days of our lives. We are not to retire from following Jesus or loving God and neighbor with our entire being; true disciples follow Jesus for life. But the assumed or appointed roles, offices, or positions may change with time. A biblical view of retirement needs careful balance, just like everything else. But to place undue burdens and guilt on older persons beyond reasonable expectations is just wrong. "To everything there is a time and a season," as the Bible clearly states in Ecclesiastes 3.

I discovered a few things about myself as I embraced retirement and moved to the slower lanes in life, feeling less rushed and with a new freedom to say no to things that gave me little joy or energy. Below are a few of those discoveries.

I cannot sleep in. Ever since I was trained on the farm to get up at 5, feed the chickens, and milk the cows, my body has been conditioned to wake up early and get moving. So I feel best if I get up early (maybe 6 or 6:30 nowadays, instead of 5) and take a brisk walk to take in some fresh morning air. Walking with God in the morning is still my favorite time of day. If it's raining or icy, I drive to a supermarket or Walmart and walk around inside to avoid slips and falls. My mind is at its sharpest in the early morning. Naomi and I often play tennis at 6 or so in the morning, before the Temple students are awake (we use their courts). We have kept our tennis rivalry going for over 50 years! (Let the record show that we played tennis on Naomi's 75th birthday, June 27, 2019.) We love that. Even after my knee replacement some years ago, we could still compete on the tennis court. My knee surgeon had told me that only 20% of his patients can play tennis after knee surgery, so I don't take that for granted.

I love the slower pace of mornings, when we can take time to watch the news, read the paper, eat breakfast, and not rush off to work or early morning meetings. We love doing the crossword and other puzzles to keep our brains exercised. I also enjoy regular naps after lunch. I can nap almost any time when I get drowsy, but I can't sleep in and feel good. If I sleep past 7 am, I get headaches. Dr. Honish told me that's because my brain needs oxygen, and that if I stay horizontal for too long, the low oxygen level gives me a headache. While that makes some sense, I wonder if I've always had this problem? Do other people suffer from the same lack? Is this connected in any way to my fused vertebrae at the top of my spine? Dr. Honish claims they've been fused since before I was born and that I'll have "arthritis of the neck" for the rest of my life, which I will need to manage, as it gets slowly worse with increasing age. It does bother me more and more. I am using the same neck exercises that Mama Peachey used to keep her neck from getting stiff. Aches and pains are definitely a part of aging. Mama Peachey used to say, "Getting old is not for sissies!" She lived to be 100.

The "circle of life" motif keeps slipping into my consciousness in new and unexpected ways. For example, in 2019 LMC and the bishop team asked me to step back in as "administrative support" for the team as "Bishop Emeritus," as Keith Weaver put it. I agreed, with careful stipulations that keep me from picking up active bishop responsibilities again. We'll see how that works out. Also, recently Nyah has moved in with us, so she can walk across the street to her classes as a Sophomore at Temple (2019-20 academic year). So now we have family living here again, even as we see more clearly than ever that we need to get rid of more than half of our "stuff" and move to a smaller house near our children, or we'll be the only ones left on a block full of students–hardly our retirement dream.

Speaking of Temple, we recently found ourselves deeply involved in connecting the new Charles Library with our local community residents. The library opened yesterday (August 25, 2019), and we had a private tour led by Joe Lucia, the Dean of Libraries, whom we recently got to know. Naomi, Nyah, and I have special invitations to the public dedication of the library on my birthday, September 12, a few weeks from now. We are also invited to a small, private luncheon with Steve Charles and his family from Lancaster, as well as friends, preceding the public ceremonies. It's another facet of retirement that was totally unanticipated. I could say more about Steve Charles, but let me just mention, for now, that he's a Mennonite farm boy from Lancaster turned multimillionaire entrepreneur in D.C., returning as the naming benefactor for the ten-million-dollar gift he gave to the library as a Temple alumnus and now a member of the board of trustees. While a student at Temple, he had worked part-time at MCPC. He and I have become friends and he introduced me to Joe Lucia and others. Here is the front facade of the new Charles Library, an architectural masterpiece:

This past week I took some people through the new library, including Keithon, then later Tee and his children, including Kai, and we met

Nyah there after her class. The big attraction for everyone is watching the Book Bot (robot) go to bins of books and then return the bins. My choice quote so far is from Keithon, who, at the end of our tour, while we were sharing a donut at Stella's Cafe inside the Charles, said, "This is like the Titanic on land!" I have always loved libraries. I was ecstatic about my personal connections to this new wonder in our neighborhood. I posted a lot on Facebook about it. Here is a sample:

"Okay, okay--for those who think I'm getting a bit carried away (I am) with my many posts about the new Charles Library at Temple, let me explain, then stop the library posts (for now): This library is across the street from us, so this is a huge plus for our neighborhood. This is not like any library you've ever seen before! Our granddaughter, Nyah, is a sophomore at Temple and helped move 2 million books from the old Paley Library to the new one. Our daughters and I all went to Temple. I have had years of interaction with Temple through Messiah College's Philadelphia campus and know the president well (former chancellor, Richard Englert). As a life-long educator, I'm a strong advocate of libraries, and my hat's off to Temple for investing in this new and exciting definition of the concept, at a time when libraries are struggling to survive. "

This year, we decided to give our younger grandchildren small Christmas gifts, but instead of trying to find age-appropriate gifts as they get older, we are giving a "grand prize" of a one-night sleepover at our house between Christmas and New Year for all 9 of them. They jumped and shouted for joy as we announced their group gift, so it seems like a hit. While it will take a lot of energy for a few days, it won't take as much as shopping for 9 individual gifts for each one. This may become a new tradition.

One of retirement's greatest joys for us is family. Having our children and grandchildren nearby, at the same church and scattered at various schools around the city (and one in college in New York City) is hugely gratifying. We could not have imagined or orchestrated such a scenario, but cherish it as another of God's great gifts. While we often run errands for our children or grandchildren and attend their school events, it is the kind of busyness that refreshes our spirits, even though it keeps us from downsizing and moving as soon as we might wish, or keeps me from attempting some writing projects that are still simmering on the back burners.

In 2020, the COVID-19 pandemic rocked the world. Our world as well. We suddenly spent most of our time at home, wearing masks when we went out in public, staying vaccinated, washing our hands endlessly, trying not to come into contact with people who had Covid, and isolating whenever we tested positive for the coronavirus. Church services moved online via Zoom, many buildings were shuttered, and life came to a deadly halt that lasted for several years. People worked from home, if possible, and whole new lifestyles evolved as everyone found ways to cope and stay alive. It was also a time of endless conspiracy theories and miracle cures. Chaos and fear ruled the growing social media networks. People disagreed passionately about whom to believe and how to behave. Our country became deeply divided on the role of government in our lives.

Interacting as families became a challenge. How to do funerals, weddings, anniversary parties, and other social events without spreading coronavirus became a daunting challenge. As one example among many, here is how we dealt with a birthday in the middle of the pandemic.

This week, for Dorian's fourteenth birthday, we took a card, a balloon, a gift card, and homemade cinnamon rolls to their house, but handed them to her from the sidewalk as we sang "Happy Birthday" from a distance. Then, in the evening, our entire family — spanning our four homes — joined a Facebook video chat and had a fun time at our "virtual party" for her. Such is life now in the middle of the global pandemic. Who can predict how long it will last or what the "new normal" will look like on the other side? Lord, have mercy on your people around the globe!

I stopped attending LMC Bishop Board meetings soon after I retired. At one time, retired bishops were invited to still attend the meetings, able to participate in discussions but without a vote. Eventually, retiree attendance seemed to dwindle and then cease. My one lasting connection with the LMC bishops is the bimonthly breakfast meeting of retired bishops in the Lancaster area. We enjoy meeting early in the morning at a restaurant, with no agenda other than eating, sharing stories, prayers, and encouragement in our retirement journeys. Currently, there are about ten of us.

I keep thinking I'm done with this chapter on retirement, ready to wrap it up. But then something else happens, often seemingly momentous. At some point, this memoir needs to end, even if life goes on. How will I know when to quit? During this self-imposed "quarantine" at home, we are going through many old files, papers, and books, finding fragments of bygone years that would be interesting to add to our story. But life is a sorting and balancing act up to the very end I guess, necessitating priorities and exclusions. Thankfully, our bodies and brains are still healthy enough to continue juggling the pieces for now, and we are content. Our tennis and Scrabble games have been nicely balanced in recent days. We are blessed to be able to enjoy retirement together.

In 2021, we moved to Discher Street in the northeast section of Philadelphia. After forty-plus years near Temple on Carlisle Street, this was a major move for us. Here is a summary from a journal entry I wrote:

<u>Thursday, June 10, 2021</u>

We have moved. After 41 amazing years at 2027 N. Carlisle Street, near Temple University, on Cinco de Mayo (May 5, 2021) Two Men and a Truck moved most of our large, heavy pieces to 5415 Discher Street, next door to Rhonda, Bryan, and Keithon. Before and after that day, we moved things in our car and other family vehicles bit by bit for a series of weeks that began to feel like months. The hectic days of packing, loading, cleaning, transporting, unpacking, and settling into our new home are finally slowing down a bit, so I might have time to write a few reflections at last.

This major move has dominated and sapped most of our time and energy, but we love that our new street is quiet, residential, and filled with families, retired folks, and children. After the noisy hustle and bustle of Broad Street and being totally surrounded by Temple students and empty Temple buildings for the past few years, this is a welcome retreat. We are slowly realizing that downsizing from 2200 square feet to 1300 square feet makes the transition feel painful and almost impossible at times. It's a great time to decide on what's really important and what is essential to keep. The flip side, of course, is letting go of all those other things.

Let's note here the fact that the Carlisle Street house was the first and only house we ever owned in our 55 years of marriage--until now. Let's also note that we hope this will be the last time we have to go house shopping and moving! It's complicated and draining. As a wise poet once said, "I just want to live in a house by the side of the road, and be a friend to man." That captures my sentiments for now.

We call this our inner-city version of the Amish "Doddy Haus" concept. It is so special to live next door to our children and youngest grandchild, Keithon. Janelle and Tee's family is exactly two blocks away, so we can easily walk to their house this weekend to feed and water Curry, their friendly dog, while they are camping. Gwen and Hector's family is about fifteen minutes away on Water Street, and we are about the same distance from Oxford Circle Mennonite, the church we all attend these days, and where Tee was recently chosen as the new Outreach Pastor. So this is all "better than it gets," as Gerry Keener would say, and we feel incredibly fortunate and blessed. It is a retirement scenario we could not have imagined: all of us living in Philadelphia rowhouses, near each other and our church.

As a retired church leader, father, husband, and grandfather, I do not take any of this for granted. To have our family all engaged in the same church and its outreach ministries–a multicultural church in the heart of the city with a holistic approach to ministry–these are retirement blessings I could not have imagined nor designed. I humbly, gratefully accept them as gifts from our benevolent God, who guides and directs us as we walk with him in the city.

I have often taught courses and seminars on "Walking with God in the city." Whenever people consider entering a city to engage in urban ministry, fear can cloud the most important kingdom truth: we are never alone in the city. God walks with us every day and everywhere. On my morning walks, I know God is walking with me, as we chat together about the issues of the day. As Jesus told Paul in Acts 18: 9 - 10, "Do not be afraid, . . . I am with you. I have many people in this city." God is at work in every city and gives us the privilege of being his coworkers as the gospel transforms lives through the power of the Holy Spirit.

And that, dear friends, is what I think God is up to in this world: creating a forever family from every language, tribe, and nation, preparing us to be multicultural neighbors in the greatest city of all time, the New Jerusalem. He invites all of us to become part of his eternal family, to find our seats at the banquet hall of the Lamb, and to experience ongoing creative expression that we cannot even imagine here on our broken planet. The fact that he has allowed me and our family, as part of his urban people garden, to have a small part in spreading that good news, handing out invitations to "whosoever will" in the City of Brotherly Love, fills me with deep gratitude. All glory to God!

EPILOGUE: QUAKERS AND SKYSCRAPERS

During my retirement years, I wanted to remain resident and engaged in the city, choosing which things to be involved in and which things to let go of. I got off the boards and committees I was on, but continued to teach or preach by request on occasion. I also volunteered from time to time. For example, I serve on the usher team at church, and joined a history committee as our church did a 75th-anniversary project recently. We collected stories from our church's history. I conducted some interviews and helped gather archival materials. I tried to prioritize those things that bring me joy or revive my spirit, realizing that I needed to slow down.

Soon after I retired, an unexpected opportunity arose: I joined the staff of the Friends Center in the heart of Philadelphia, near City Hall.

For years, as we lived in North Philadelphia, and as I worked with churches and ministries all across the city and beyond, while teaching courses at Messiah College Philadelphia Campus by Temple University, I could clearly see the skyscrapers standing tall and strong in the heart of the city, just a short drive down Broad Street from our house. I often wondered what it would feel like to work among the skyscrapers (having gotten to know Willard Rouse III, who built the One and Two Liberty Place towers), meeting people from all over the world in that bustling central business district, literally a crossroads of the world.

God must have been listening to my unspoken musings. Soon after I retired, I read about an opportunity to apply for a front-desk job at the Friends Center, "The Quaker Hub for Peace and Justice in Philadelphia," just a few blocks from all those skyscrapers! I applied and was hired. I have been working there part-time ever since. It seemed like the perfect fit. As a part-time evening and weekend desk clerk, I get to meet many interesting people from near and far, some just passing through, while others are on staff with the 40 organizations renting space in our office building. Additionally, dozens of groups rent space at the center for meetings, conferences, training events, and more. Occasionally, I work the front desk on a Sunday morning while the Quakers meet for silent worship in the large meetinghouse at the center of our campus. In many ways, I get to interact with people from all over the world and get paid a modest part-time wage for doing so! I enjoy my work so much that I would do it as an unpaid volunteer, but the extra cash helps with fixed-income retirement living–an added bonus.

When I began working there, I was told that "Quakers don't proselytize," so I was not to try to convince anyone to become a Quaker. But so many people came in asking, "What is this place? Who are the Quakers? Is this a church?" that I asked for printed information to hand out when I had to answer such inquiries. I was given brochures explaining Quaker beliefs and practices, which I began handing out. I also explained the Sunday-morning silent worship meeting in our large meetinghouse, which they were most welcome to attend. That usually satisfied my curious customers, who appreciated succinct explanations. Was I "proselytizing"? The inside joke at the Friends Center became, "Our retired Mennonite bishop does our evangelism for us!" When people find out that I'm a Mennonite, they often say, "If I weren't a Quaker, I'd probably be a Mennonite." And I often reply that the reverse might be true for me as well.

Mennonites and Quakers–both historic peace churches–have worked together for peace and justice around the world for many years, so it feels natural to work together. We may have some differences in worship, theology, and practices, but we share a deep belief in "that of God in everyone," that every human bears the divine image and is worthy of deep love and respect, that peace and justice go hand in hand, and that violence and war are never the answer. We believe that word and deed go hand in hand. Quakers and Mennonites in Philadelphia wrote the first religious protest against slavery in America in 1688. Germantown Mennonite Church still has the desk, reportedly the one on which the document was signed.

I also remember that when my first Miller ancestor arrived at Penns Landing in Philadelphia, he walked seven miles north to Germantown and settled with the Quakers and Mennonites, who worked and worshiped together for some years in what is now Germantown, fully incorporated into the city. His walk was on the cowpath that is now Germantown Avenue, which connects many diverse communities of Philadelphia, from Chestnut Hill to Penns Landing. This realization became a huge full-circle moment for me, a parable or metaphor of my life. Somehow, I embody this entire history in my heart and soul in an almost unimaginable way. I try to embrace that reality every day as a gift. As Walt Whitman famously wrote, "I am vast. I contain multitudes."

When I'm working at the front desk of the Friends Center, I keep an eye on the doors, the computer, the events calendar, the security cameras, and monitor all who come and go, making sure they know which room or office to go to, which meeting is happening in which space, and answer the office phone. I welcome all who enter, answer questions and address complaints, direct visitors, and ensure that no one with ill intent enters the premises, so that, in general, all things run smoothly throughout the campus. When I lock up at night, I have to check all floors, lock all security doors, set the alarms, and lock the entrance gates on the sidewalk. As I do so, I look up at those brightly-lit skyscrapers nearby and think, "What is this Amish farmboy doing among the skyscrapers?"

Perhaps that is the connecting theme of my life: farming. Rural farming, urban farming, global farming. God told humans from the very beginning to "tend to the garden." In other words, take care of the habitat where you live. Our habitat for the moment is Planet Earth. We are all trying to take care of the little corner where we live, from mowing the lawn to dusting the piano, washing the dishes, or sweeping up the leaves and debris along the sidewalk. I often think of the urban church as "God's People Garden," affecting the neighborhood and the city as salt, light, and yeast, all metaphors for the Kingdom that Christ came to inaugurate when he visited Planet Earth in the flesh. Our ministries, as ambassadors for Christ, are also incarnational. Moving into the neighborhood is transformative.

Skyscrapers are part of the built urban environment, where people live and work to make the world a better place. Every morning, someone gets up, puts the coffee on, feeds the cat and the kids, then goes off to work in a corner office of one of those gleaming glass towers, planning how to make that skyscraper work all day smoothly, serving the hundreds of people working or doing business in that building. That is very much like the farmer–Amish or otherwise–who gets up and starts farming all over again every morning, growing food for the teeming multitudes. As the Christian urbanist, Ray Bakke, often says, "The Bible begins in a garden, but it ends up in a city. You have an urban future, whether you like it or not!" Something to embrace and prepare for here and now. See you there!

ENDORSEMENTS FROM MY GRANDCHILDREN

For my 83rd birthday in 2025, my grandchildren surprised me on a Sunday by calling me up front after our worship service at Oxford Circle Mennonite Church and said they wanted to give me a gift for my birthday: a special single-issue newspaper they had created just for the occasion. The back page was filled with tributes by each grandchild (see next two pages). The front page contained the title, *The Urban Menno*, and a fake, made-up story about my becoming a professional tennis player (Naomi and I have played tennis for over 50 years) after retiring as a bishop. It was hilarious, heartfelt, and deeply moving, the best gift ever!

You have a gift of seeing what each person brings to the table. Thank you for seeing that in all of your grandchildren, whether they're 2 years old or 20. It made my voice feel valuable, even when I was only talking about my farm at Temple haha. Kai

* * *

Happy birthday Grandpa! I love visiting you and hearing all your stories and knowledge on the many things that are going on in this crazy world. I know I can always count on you for encouragement and answers to my questions. I can't wait to celebrate many more birthdays with you! Love, Dori

* * *

When we first met, I think you took a candid photo of me. I didn't expect it then, but have learned that it's normal for you to capture spontaneous moments of your family. I've watched you photograph birthday parties, vacations, and even simple living room chats- all showing just how much you love your family. Thank you for including me in these memories and making me feel welcomed from the start. Dom

* * *

Hearing all your stories, I can tell that you have had both an eventful and blessed life thus far. Thank you for sharing it with us and I hope this newspaper is a demonstration of our appreciation for your stories. I also admire the love you have for our family and how proud you are to share it with others. Thanks for being a wise, thoughtful, and loving grandpa. Amari

* * *

Happy birthday Grandpa! You have shown me so much of what it means to follow Christ and make Him known to people. You inspire me to keep learning, exploring, and reading in order to truly take in all that this world has to offer. I love how much you appreciate music, and all that you have taught me about it. Thank you for being so kind, caring and empathetic, you set a very good example for all of us grandchildren. I love you Grandpa! Zayah

* * *

Grandpa, every time I come to you and grandma's house, you always have a story or a fact to share. You are the person equivalent of a newspaper. I love hearing them and I love you. Happy bday! -Sincerely, the youngest

grand-pa /gran(d), PiV
noun

1. *one's <u>grandfather</u>.*
2. *the man who sits you down on a stool when you're acting up, and tells you to "take a break."*
3. *the patriarch of the family who feeds your curiosity with stories, songs, and ideas.*
4. *the one who taught you to love the word of the Lord.*
5. *the visionary who left his home to pursue the voice calling him to "tend to my sheep."*
6. *a well of wisdom whose roots run deep.*
7. *someone whose infectious joy outpaces the weight of the world.*
8. *the one responsible for who I am today.*
9. *my grandpa. Jaron*

* * *

It always amazes me how you seem to know everything about everything (as well as everyone). From knowing stats for Phillies players to some random fact about a long lost German ancestor, I feel like I always learn something in every conversation we have. I hope to one day become a walking encyclopedia too. I think it shows your love for knowledge and you're always so excited to share it. I think you've made us all smarter because of it hehe. Happy birthday! Nyah

* * *

Happy birthday Grandpa! Thank you so much for all of the wisdom you've imparted into my life. I would not be who I am today without you. I look forward to many more theological discussions and conversations about random stuff I'm learning in school. I love and appreciate you so much, and I hope and pray to celebrate many more birthdays with you! Your favorite seventeen year-old grandson

* * *

HAPPY BIRTHDAY GRANDPA!!!!! I love you so much and I hope that you had a great birthday and loved all of the surprises that occurred. I am so grateful for all of the things that you have taught me over these 83 years (like goofy german words) and I hope that you can teach me so much more. I love you so much and I couldn't have asked for a better grandpa. Brielle

ABOUT THE AUTHOR

Freeman J. Miller and his family have lived and worked in Philadelphia for over 50 years. Freeman served as pastor at Diamond Street Mennonite Church, taught at Messiah College Philadelphia Campus, and was bishop of the Philadelphia District of LMC for 15 years. He also directed EMM's Home Ministries Department from a Philadelphia base for 3 years. During that time, he worked with church planters from Maine to Mississippi. His wife, Naomi, was Ron Sider's administrative assistant at Palmer Seminary for 27 years. They raised their three daughters in North Philadelphia and are now living close to them and their families in the Oxford Circle area of Philadelphia. Most of them attend Oxford Circle Mennonite Church. Even though Freeman grew up Amish, his passion is for the multicultural urban church, which he sees as a key vehicle for carrying out Christ's Great Commission in a rapidly urbanizing world, focusing on the church in Antioch (Acts 13) as an excellent New Testament model. Their 9 grandchildren, and one great-grandchild, all living nearby, give Freeman and Naomi great joy. In his retirement years, Freeman likes to read, write, cheer on the Phillies and Eagles, study cities, play tennis and Scrabble with Naomi, and work part-time for the Quakers at the Friends Center in the heart of Philadelphia. Email: urbanmenno@gmail.com.